NO LUCKS GIVEN.

Life is hard, but there is hope

By

Brother Marcellus Luck IV
with Marcus Costantino

You are not alone!

No Lucks Given LLC
Colorado Springs, CO

No Lucks Given LLC

321 N. Tejon Street

Colorado Springs, CO 80903

ISBN: 978-0-578-39781-8

Cover Design by Lea Flores

Cover Illustration copyright © No Lucks Given LLC. All rights reserved.

Editing by Cristina Wright

Interior layout by Ben Wolf (www.benwolf.com/editing-services)

First Printing: 2022

Printed in The United States of America

To Tina, my beautiful wife

Love is patient, love is kind. It does not envy, it does not boast, it is not proud. It does not dishonor others, it is not self-seeking, it is not easily angered, it keeps no record of wrongs. Love does not delight in evil but rejoices with the truth. It always protects, always trusts, always hopes, always perseveres. Love never fails.

CONTENTS

FOREWORD

I first met Brother Luck in 2006 during the twentieth anniversary celebration of the Park Hyatt Masters of Food and Wine in Carmel, CA. I was assigned an assistant to help prepare for the weekend's extensive itinerary and, focused on executing my signature dishes for more than 250 people, I appreciated the extra pair of hands. I didn't get to know my young assistant well that day - but I do remember his enthusiasm, curiosity, and willingness to learn.

Years later, at a charity event in Manhattan, I was approached by that same chef. Grown now, and looking like an NFL linebacker, Brother reminded me of our time together in Carmel. He told me he had purchased his own plane ticket and volunteered his time at that event, years ago, with the specific hope of working alongside me in the kitchen. I was humbled to hear he was an alumnus of C-CAP (Careers through Culinary Arts Program), an organization dear to me, of which I have been a co-chair for many years. It provides high-school-aged teenagers with culinary training and a pathway to success through cooking, with a specific focus on the importance of mentorship.

The mission of C-CAP reflects my own journey. The training and guidance I received from my own teachers in Sweden was a major catalyst that helped ignite my passion for cooking and for connecting with people over good food. I am committed to passing along that same care and professional investment that I received by encouraging young chefs' development and helping them succeed in both life and work. I am so proud to affirm that Brother Luck is one of C-CAP's success stories, and that he applies his amazing energy, drive, and focus to changing our industry for the better.

It's been a joy to follow Brother's journey of becoming a business owner, television personality, and, most importantly, a mentor to others. I love how he thinks outside the box in order to facilitate positive change. For instance, he has fostered a relationship with a local military base and trains their cooks in his restaurants, which is a brilliant and resourceful way to both serve the community and bolster the restaurant industry as we face labor shortages. And recently, Brother implemented Sober Week for his restaurant teams. He organized and hosted a week-long series of activities including yoga, hiking, and kickball to interrupt what can often be a toxic restaurant lifestyle. Brother models life-change by choosing to refrain from alcohol, and he invests his money, time, and energy into setting an example for his team to do the same.

Brother has endured many hardships in his life, and he has overcome them in great part because he was inspired and guided by many people. This book shares many of the stories of his mentors—some good and some bad. There is much to be learned from this man's life. His message is one of hope and perseverance, courage and determination.

Each time I cross paths with Brother, I reflect on the man he is becoming and smile, inspired by his mindset and grateful for his approach to changing the industry I love. Brother's willingness to be open and vulnerable, especially in the workplace and on social media, is refreshing and inspiring. He's just getting started and I'm excited to see how his journey continues to unfold as a great chef and wonderful storyteller. I'm thrilled he's finally sharing his story with all of you.

- Marcus Samuelsson

INTRODUCTION

As iron sharpens iron, so one person sharpens another.

Life is hard: a few years ago, I joined a men's group. It seemed to have a singular purpose: learn what your story is and research your personal history and timeline to understand why you make the decisions you do. We used a book as our guide: *Wild at Heart.* I was by far the youngest member of the group, but I felt out of place not because I was thirty years behind most of these guys but because they were going to be out of touch with the realities of my world and, more significantly, me. I assumed they wouldn't know how to relate to me and my background of growing up in the streets, fighting for everything I had, and working so hard to get to where I was at. So, as the weeks passed, with low expectations, I would hit them with stories just to see their reactions. And there was a significant amount of shock because I've gone through it; I've had a lot of crazy things happen in my life.

But the magnitude of surprise was not a one-way street. By the end of our time together, I had learned all of us were navigating much the same thing. We were all sharing the same emotions and dealing with similar realities: fear, anxiety, depression, not feeling wanted, isolation, and the pressure of trying to be a leader of a tribe without having any idea of how to lead or where we were going. We all felt this, and we were hiding it. Each of us was creating and presenting an image of whom we wanted others to think we were. I learned I was not alone in keeping people at arm's length—outside of my inner circle—and, more importantly, outside of me. My thinking? "You're never going to get to know the real me."

This discovery—there is a common thread of emotions and posturing in the lives of people—led to a season of change in which I realized I was disconnecting myself from people. In the midst of my loneliness, I was lamenting how I wasn't getting invites to go to parties, BBQs, or social events. I asked my wife, "Why doesn't anyone call me anymore? Why don't I have any friends?"

"You created that," she explained.

It hit me hard. I had created a perception that I was too busy. I chose to be isolated. I chose to be alone because it was easier. As I got deeper into the discussion, I began to realize my self-isolating stemmed from my past.

Many people in my life have broken my trust. I don't know when it happened, but at some point, after opening myself up and being vulnerable with others—bringing them into my world, introducing them to my family and my feelings, and giving them myself—I just stopped. How many times can you have your trust broken and just keep trusting? Inevitably, after too many relational curveballs, you just stop swinging. You shut down. You stop playing. You build a wall so thick that nobody will get through it. That's a survivalist mentality. That's a sense of desperation, which leads toward self-preservation. I'm in defense mode. I'm in survival mode. I'm going to make it no matter what comes at me. I'll get through it. I'm going to suffer through the pain, and I'll keep standing here and fighting.

That mentality was born in me when my father passed away—when I lost my male role model. I was supposed to become the image of my dad. And when I lost him, all of a sudden snatched and gone in a week, at only ten years old, I became the man of the house. Overnight, I had to become an adult. I found myself in situations of abuse, neglect, and hunger, and I had to fight. I had to protect myself and my brother.

The people we were around wanted to make us tougher. When you live in a rough neighborhood, everything is about being hard, being tough, and presenting an image of strength and self-sufficiency. It was common for us to get beaten up by well-meaning cousins and friends to make us tougher. Repeatedly punching an eleven-year-old boy to make him tougher isn't right, but it is what it is. There were times when my brother would be going through the same thing. I would have to jump in and help. We always ended up catching a beat down together.

Abuse is one of the worst things you can do to a child. But in that environment, you don't know any better because the mentality of lower-income neighborhoods and troubled areas is so often all about survival. The anxiety and fear are constant because there is a sense that if you have something someone else wants, they are just going to take it. You better be prepared to protect it. It's gut-wrenching. And I spent all of the years between my father's passing and adulthood living in that mentality, numbing the pain through drugs and violence and nonsense. I didn't know I was numbing myself. I didn't know I was in that much pain. I was disconnected. I was protecting myself.

I was sixteen when I got into culinary, and it wasn't because I wanted to be a chef or go on Food Network; it was because I was hungry, and they would give me a steak sandwich at lunch. I couldn't afford to buy a meal. That's what got me into culinary.

A lot of people ask me how I found my passion—my career—so early. It was in the kitchen that, for the first time since my father died, I had a male role model give me positive reinforcement. He complimented me. I became so addicted to the attention; I wanted more. I craved more; I worked for it. I was good at cooking because they told me I was good at cooking. And I started to believe them.

As I've progressed in life—spiritually, emotionally, personally, and professionally—I've never forgotten that message. And I want to have that same impact on other young adults. And because our lives are not as dissimilar as we assume—we've all got a story, we've all got a struggle—we can make a difference in someone's life if we choose to. Everyone has a story. Most of us have learned from our stories. But we downplay our stories because we don't think they are important enough, or we believe other stories are better or worse. What is fascinating is someone needs to hear your story because it will change their life. They probably went through something very similar to what you went through or have a background that's eerily familiar to your own. And you have to share your story; you need to talk about the loneliness, anger, and pain because somebody's going to connect to it. It could be a moment in their life that shifts their path from depression and suicidal thoughts to hope.

It seems like everyone's on Instagram: everyone's on Facebook. And all we're doing is posting our greatest hits—the highlight reel of our lives, right now. People are measuring themselves against it, believing, "Oh, I got to be like that," and "That's the chef I want to be like." People are being set up for failure because they are never going to create a life that looks like your cool dinners, amazing trips, and the beautiful people you hang out with. You know you hang out with regular people, you eat crappy fast food, you have hangovers where you hide all day in your pajamas, but nobody's talking about that side of life. We're showing a glamorous lifestyle that doesn't exist. That's why I'm opening up on social media and sharing the ugly as well as the beautiful.

This book tells my story of finding God and learning to love and value family, all while embracing my passion for food. While it might be considered my memoir, more importantly, it is about you. What is your story? What is your faith? What is motivating you? I promise to tell you more about me as long as you promise to think more about you.

The band of brothers, Mike Epstein, Casey Fink, Brian Franks, Joe Gungler, and Brother Luck are off to spend some guy time in New Orleans.

1. THE MOMENT I KNEW

If you faint in the day of adversity, your strength is small.

Not long after my thirtieth birthday, I stood center stage, feeling the burn of the lights hanging directly over my head. I feel like the prime rib I saw on the buffet station the night before at my hotel. I'm looking Bobby Flay directly in the eye as we stand toe to toe. I keep telling myself, "Don't break eye contact." He needs to realize the type of warrior he's about to battle, and he's not intimidating anyone. I take a deep breath and embrace reality; I plan on sticking a knife in Bobby Flay in his own kitchen.

I'm feeling nauseous. My mouth feels parched, and I can't stop sweating. My black dress shirt is soaked from running around the cooking studio for the last two hours. I wish I had worn my chef coat since it's way more comfortable and breathable, but the producers requested I wear this stupid dress shirt. I'm irritated I've ruined a nice shirt. We're in the middle of filming *Beat Bobby Flay,* and I think I've got a solid shot at winning. I knocked out the first contestant after a chicken wing challenge, and now I'm getting the chance to battle Bobby.

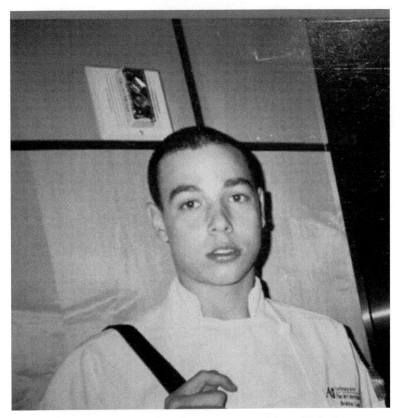

A nervous Brother Luck (age 17) waits to compete in Atlanta, GA, for the national best teen chef competition, where he would win a full scholarship. (2000)

"Alright, Brother Luck, you're gonna need some serious luck in round two," says Flay with a smirk. "What is your signature dish tonight?"

I calmly respond, "My signature dish is Pulled Pork Sliders," knowing this isn't the dish he was expecting.

Bobby's facial expressions are a sure tell he's none too excited about the idea of cooking pulled pork sliders in less than an hour. He looks directly at me and says, "Really? Pulled pork in forty-five minutes?"

The live crowd oohs in suspense as one of the judges, Elvis Duran, remarks to Bobby Flay, "You look nervous." Bobby is giving me more and more confidence by the second as he openly wears his frustration on his face. I'm laughing internally because I distinctly remember having very similar feelings when the show's casting team asked me if I could cook pulled pork in forty-five minutes. My immediate response was laughter, followed by, "It can't be done in such a short amount of time." A good pulled pork shoulder needs to be cooked low and slow for twelve hours. If you have any type of common sense, you would be asking the same question I'm asking myself. How did I end up on the set of a national television show, challenging one of the most iconic chefs to an impossible cooking challenge?

I want to beat him and will have to use every trick up my sleeve to topple the Iron Chef. The judges are creating the perfect distraction because they continuously tease Bobby Flay as we're cooking. I begin working on my barbecue sauce, and one of the judges, Katie Lee, yells across the set, "Brother Luck, it smells good!"

Bobby immediately retorts in a mock childish voice, "Brother Luck, it smells so good!"

I can't believe I'm cooking against Bobby Flay, and he's frustrated! I used to watch him on *Iron Chef* when I was a teenager, and it's surreal going head-to-head with him to see who has, on this day, the better skills. I'm working on my sauce and trying to find balance within the flavors. How's the sweetness? Does it need more mustard? What about a touch of apple cider vinegar?

Katie Lee walks over to Bobby's station and asks to try his sauce. I look up from my cutting board just in time to see her facial expression as she reacts to the taste. She laughs and says, "It's really spicy. You should leave it just as is."

When you're making any sauce, it's tough to dilute spicy while maintaining a good flavor. I smirked, thinking, "Bobby Flay just got a little heavy-handed with his iconic peppers, and now I have an opening to win this epic culinary showdown." That was the moment I knew.

During the final moments of our allotted cooking time, I focus on flavor. I cool the pressure cooker with cold water and prepare for the moment of truth. Will the pork be tender in only thirty minutes? I release the steam and open the lid of the pressure cooker to find a tender and flavorful pot of pork shoulder. I've done it! I've achieved what most said couldn't be done, and now I just need to finish strong. I want my dish to be very similar to his style of food, so I char some pineapple and crumble some Mexican cheese into my slaw. I taste the meat and realize it needs just a touch more smoke flavor. Earlier in the round, I had noticed a smoking gun that could be used to impart wood smoke flavor. I place the pulled pork into a mixing bowl and cover it with plastic wrap. I fill the chamber of the smoking gun with applewood sawdust and light it on fire. The hose sends billows of smoke directly into my pork, adding much-needed complementary flavor. I shake the bowl a few times to incorporate the smoke and begin my final plating. I grab some wooden planks from the shelves of plate options and cross my fingers as time runs out. Hopefully, this is the dish that will beat Bobby Flay.

Standing under these stage lights reminds me of a child playing with a magnifying glass on a sunny day. I can feel the heat radiating off my ears, forehead, and shoulders. I can't stop sweating. I'm using a napkin to continuously dab my face as we listen to the judges' critiques. My poker face never falters as the judges blindly taste our dishes. Every time one of them comments on a flavor or ingredient, I don't move a muscle. I don't want to give any indications as to which dish was mine or influence their decision. We're only a few minutes away from finding out who won this battle. The judges begin to tally their sheets and make their final choice on who prepared the best pulled pork slider. Katie Lee silently looks at both of us and begins to announce the decision from the judges. "And the winner of the Fourth of July pulled pork slider competition is...Brother Luck!"

Holy shit! I just Beat Bobby Flay on his own show. That was

the first synapsis firing in my brain as I came to grips with what just happened.

I smile with a sense of relief and look directly into the audience, searching for my wife, Tina. The moment we make eye contact, and I see the look on her face, it confirms this is really happening. I just Beat Bobby Flay! I just made pulled pork in forty-five minutes! I take a deep breath, and my shoulders finally come out of my ears.

My name is Chef Brother Luck, and I just beat Bobby Flay.

Brother and Tina Luck. (2015)

2. SHATTERED SOUL

If one curses his father or his mother,
his lamp will be put out in utter darkness.

Every young child has joy; they know nothing else. It's raw, and it's innocent. But that innocence is all too often tainted by narcissistic people, stressful situations, and lies, lies, and more lies. In his book *Wild at Heart*, John Eldredge explains what I now know to be true: "Every man carries a wound. I have never met a man without one. No matter how good your life may have seemed to you, you live in a broken world full of broken people."[1]

My story begins with joy. My mom and dad raised my younger brother, Slade, and me in the San Francisco Bay Area. In the '80s, San Francisco was a fantastic city offering arts, culture, enterprise, and some of the world's best food (mainly in Chinatown). I loved growing up in the city. There was an energy that came from all the people living in the row houses, kids playing on the sidewalks and in the streets, and the hills—I loved the hills.

After the 1989 earthquake, we moved to Los Angeles. I remember getting my hands dirty in my aunt's backyard garden and the stickiness of fresh pomegranate dripping down my chin.

And I have a vivid memory of walking with her through a farmers' market for the first time and seeing the big bushels of collard greens and perfectly ripe tomatoes. We went to Disneyland and Universal Studios. We visited the beach as often as we could. My dad's family surrounded us, and all seemed to be right in the world. I had a fun childhood until we moved back to Vallejo in 1993. Within the year, my dad died; our lives were turned upside down.

My parents were going through a divorce shortly before my father passed away. I remember taking the BART train to spend the weekend with my mother and then heading back to spend the school week with my father. I was stuck in the middle. I despised waiting in the lobby at the divorce lawyer's office; I still hate the smell of wood polish.

I like to think they would have worked it out, but deep in my heart, I know the truth. It was over. They had grown apart, and Slade and I were stuck in the middle. Had my dad not died, I know we would not have been spared the pain of the vicious emotional cycle that goes along with parents divorcing.

I remember sitting on my top bunk crying as my legs dangled through the fire-engine-red safety bar. My ten-year-old mind had just made a tough decision. Moving forward, I wanted to live with my father. If faced with the choice of which parent to choose, I was going to go with him. I felt guilty about it, and I'm sure my disconnectedness from my mom is long connected to my guilt.

It wasn't as if she had done anything wrong—I loved my mom. The feelings were more along the lines of "I'm a boy, and I need to be raised by a man." I respected and admired my father. He was very strict but always provided me with reasons why. He held me accountable for everything I did, or at least what he caught me doing. When he suddenly passed, everything I had envisioned about the future changed. I was struck with the grief that only a child who's lost a parent knows.

"Wake up, honey. Please wake up, son," my mother pleaded as she roused me from a deep sleep. My eyes crept open—revealing her angelic face—as an internal alarm sounded inside my soul, screaming something was wrong. I jumped off my pillow, ready and alert, noticing tears in her bright crystal blue eyes. Her hand trembled as she stroked my face softly with a mother's touch.

"I need you to wake your brother and come to my room," she said as she slowly disappeared into the hallway.

I scrambled out of my bed and realized it was the middle of the night. What was going on? Why was she crying? I stirred my seven-year-old brother from his childhood dreams, gently saying, "Wake up, Slade. Come on. Mom needs us."

As we ghostly walked into our parents' bedroom and crawled onto their massive king-sized bed, my mother embraced us both in a hug tighter than ever. She began crying and whispered, "Your father died tonight in the hospital, and he's gone." Squeezing tighter—revealing her disbelief—she kept saying, "He's just gone."

My ten-year-old brain tried to process what my mother had just told us. What did she mean our father was gone and not coming back? Did she say *died* as in forever? The pain crept in and morphed into horror. I had just lost the most important person in my life, and he was never coming back. My father was not coming back from the hospital. He wasn't going to get better and come home. I was never going to hear that bellow of a laugh from deep within his belly while he played practical jokes on family members. I was never going to finish our embarrassing conversation about my homework on the female reproductive system. He wouldn't be there for my upcoming eleventh birthday or see me graduate into middle school. There wouldn't be any more dancing in the living room as we lifted weights listening to his old vinyl records. I was never going to have another conversation or get the fatherly advice I took for granted.

How could he be gone? What had happened in the few hours since we visited him in his hospital room and laughed while watching *Are You Being Served* on BBC?

What had I done wrong to deserve this? Was it because I was bad, and this was my punishment? What did the doctors do wrong? Was God playing a cruel joke on me?

With my adolescent mind so overwhelmed, all I could do was curl up in a ball next to the only family I had left and cry. Slade, at first not understanding why we were woken up in the middle of the night, quickly understood the implication of the word *died* after seeing my reaction to mom's words and my ensuing tears.

Only a few months earlier, all of our Christmas toys had been hidden under a blanket on top of the bed we were crouched upon. The pain led to tears, the tears to exhaustion, and the exhaustion to sleep. The worst day of my life would haunt me for years: the day my dad died.

My Father: Brother Marcellus Haywood Luck III. (1947-1994)

My father experienced more life in his forty-six years than most people lived in one hundred years. He was an exotic dancer who traveled the world without worry or apprehension until my giant nine-pound seven-ounce self came into this world on August 20, 1983. He majored in drama and dreamed of becoming a professional wrestler in the World Wrestling Federation, entertaining the masses alongside the likes of Hulk Hogan.

I liked watching my dad shave and get ready for work. I would examine his face and see his smile. Looking into the mirror, I would rub my chin and wonder when I would grow some stubble and get to use his can of Magic Shaving Powder. On this day, while I was standing beside him, he suddenly became ill, coughing violently and vomiting specks of blood into the toilet.

"Dad? Dad! Are you ok?" I cried between the hacking. "Are you okay to go to work today?"

"I'm fine, son. Don't you worry," he calmly replied, wiping his face.

And with that, he went to work, and I went to school.

He had recently started a new position working as a nurse for the St. Jude Hospital in Concord, California. He was working double shifts to provide the beautiful Northern California townhome we were living in. My parents ensured that Slade and I had everything we needed.

Later that day, while I was learning long division and taking geography tests, my dad was admitted to the very hospital he was an employee of. It took less than a week for him to pass away and our lives to be turned upside down with grief.

I don't remember crying at his funeral, probably because I kept wishing he would wake up and crawl out of the casket laughing about the greatest prank he had ever pulled, but that never happened. He really was gone forever.

When we returned home for the wake, I sat on the carpeted bottom step outside his bedroom, rocking myself into catalepsy. I couldn't stop crying, and I felt so angry he was taken from me. As the tears poured from my soul, all I wished for was for Dad to find me and tell me it was all a bad dream. I sat with my arms folded and my head cradled between my knees, watching a puddle of tears stain the carpet when an arm suddenly wrapped around my shoulders. Through my wet eyes, I saw Pastor Aaron, the preacher who had delivered my father's eulogy. Pastor Aaron was a young man, and I remembered him from my mother's old church back in Los Angeles. He opened his Bible and asked if I would pray with him while he read some verses. After a few minutes of reading the Bible together, a rage awakened within me. I shook my head at God for taking my father and vowed to never feel that pain again. This grudge toward God would haunt me for years to come. I labored to build monstrous towering walls around my shattered heart. I see now how that day marked the beginning of my transformation from a young boy to an isolated and lonely man.

For a long time, I lived with the pain of being angry with God for taking my father away. How does an almighty and powerful God allow so much pain to occur in his world? Why doesn't he ease the pain and start making things right? Death, violence, neglect, abuse, shame, and fear haunted my dreams and memories. I didn't know if it would ever end.

Some years later, my uncle told me my father was only a few days away from gaining benefits from his employer, which would have provided life insurance to cover the funeral costs. Under those unique circumstances, our family petitioned the insurance company only to be denied. Today, as a business owner, I understand the importance of caring for our employees and being gracious in the midst of their personal lives, which can, on any given day without warning, be turned inside-out.

Who knows how my story would have played out if my father

had been granted his life insurance, ensuring my widowed mother had financial security for her children. I'll always keep that as a reminder of how one individual's decision has the power to drastically change someone's life.

My mother eventually told me Dad had been diagnosed HIV positive in the late eighties and had been taking black market medication for the symptoms. (She assured me none of us had been exposed, and we all took a blood test to confirm it.) Some who knew him believe those medications, combined with the treatment he was receiving for his illness, caused his heart to stop. Other family members told me he had a brain aneurysm while receiving an MRI in the hospital because of his claustrophobia.

Today, even as I write this book, I don't know what caused my father's death. I don't care to find out because understanding the cause of his death will never bring him back. So what's the point? I've considered paying for his death certificate to learn what the cause of death was, but I struggle every time I attempt to order it. I don't want to dwell in the past when I can see a bright future ahead. I'm still angry; I won't deny it. But I am trying really hard to trust God with my story, my pain, and my life. For now, I'll make some assumptions about something only God knows, and I'll ask him when I get my chance.

My father passed away twenty-nine years ago, and I still can't stand the thought that he's gone. Sometimes I pretend he's just in another state. Some days, I talk to him out loud, seeking parental advice. Most days, I just strive to be a man he would be proud of.

Most importantly, I follow the values he taught me as a boy: faith, family, and food. This book is meant to be an interpretation of those topics and how I've incorporated them into my life since his passing in May 1994. I'm mindful of my journey. There are times I am so entrenched in the muck and mire that all I see is the mud around me and no path out. But there are other times I see the path ahead—the one God is making clear.

The Lord often does a curious thing when making paths straight—he uses broken men and women to love, care for, and guide other broken men and women. No matter where you are, whatever bad encircles you, whatever demon haunts you, don't go it alone. We all need help, and the best place to get help is in the form of people.

For those of you who are still broken but perhaps a little less so than you used to be, now is the time to share your life and your story with others who need to be encouraged and reminded they are loved and are not alone. You don't have to have your life in order before you start mentoring or caring for people in your life. You just have to start doing it.

I can point to countless people who have loved me, cared for me, prayed for me, and mentored me. I'm doing everything I can to follow authentic people. I'm inspired by their courage, vulnerability, and availability. I don't want to walk this street called *life* alone. I want to walk beside people, in front of people, and behind them, helping them get to where they need and want to go—just as others have done for me.

Who do you keep within your inner circle? What are you bringing to their lives? What are they bringing into yours? Is the inspiration and authenticity a two-way street? Do the people you walk with want to be a part of your life? Do you want to be a part of theirs? Friendships should always be about quality and never quantity.

None of us are alone, even in our darkest days. We can always look up and listen, and we can always find a friend.

3. THE PAIN IS REAL

Where there is no guidance the people fall,
But in abundance of counselors there is victory.

I 've had a few people in my life end their own lives.

A few years ago, my niece Samantha took her life. She was one of the most vibrant people I've ever met. We had bonded over the loss of a parent; her mother had passed away from cancer. She was about the same age as I was when my father died. She was so freaking smart. Tina and I flew to Tucson, Arizona, to watch her graduate as valedictorian. The conversations I had with my niece were not that of a teenager. She shared her aspirations and dreams. Her wounds were evident, but I never thought they were irreparable.

Samantha was so likable and charismatic. We wanted her to move to Colorado Springs and attend college. As I was hiding my depression, she was battling similar demons.

Out of nowhere, Samantha committed suicide. I was broken. Our family was shattered. No one saw it coming because she was the one least expected to give up to the pain. It made me wonder how I could have made a difference. Could I have said something?

Should I have stayed more connected to her? Could I have made more of an impact on Samantha's life? When she pulled away, why didn't I dive in?

Brother and Tina Luck with their niece Samantha Jane Turner. (2010)

Mental health struggles are real, especially among teens. Depression and suicidal thoughts are overwhelming a lot of kids and their families. It's a dark place. So many kids are disconnected from their families, friends, and faith because they are depressed. Most are ashamed of having suicidal thoughts. When you talk to them about it, you rarely get any answers because mental struggles breed isolation and loneliness. When you get into a funk, you just want to stay in that funk. You demand to be left alone. You become defiant. You push hard on the ones you love because you know they are not going anywhere and because you can. For me, it was my wife who bore the brunt of my pain. But she told me I had to do something about it. I started seeing a therapist.

Learning to be okay sitting in a counselor's office is one of the greatest things I've ever done. I quickly realized I was ready to talk. When I was a teenager, I was sent to therapy, but I didn't want to be there and reacted to just about everything with, "Whatever." But now, as an adult with deep pain, I was ready to confront many of those demons from my early years. I was ready to talk about my childhood experiences. Week after week, we examined my teenage years—story after story—broken relationships, violence, pain, anger, loneliness, and depression. It was helpful to talk about my life and work through the emotions with someone unbiased and nonjudgmental—someone who heard me and saw me. Session after session, I would sit in my car, reflecting on the conversation that had transpired.

I was realizing that I was in survival mode. I was embracing the reality that I had PTSD (Post Traumatic Stress Disorder) resulting from my childhood. Societally, we often limit the idea of PTSD to those who have served in the military, but this is happening to our youth! Children are losing their parents. Kids have friends who die. Teens live in communities surrounded by violence and are abused in their homes or beaten up on the streets. Social media has become a child's new best friend, and their reality is blurred because this friend is much more than an imaginary Drop Dead Fred. This friend is telling them all the wrong things about themselves: You're not pretty enough. You're not strong enough. You're failing at life. You're simply not good enough to exist. Every one of those dark moments sows the seed of PTSD. Without help, these kids will live the rest of their lives dealing with trauma. They will build and maintain walls to protect themselves. Seeing no alternative, they will choose not to trust anyone. I know this, personally, because I was one of those kids.

I remember a bad bout of depression. I was on a work-related trip and had become very aggressive and defiant, isolating myself from my peers. Being alone in a hotel room was not the best place for me. I wasn't surrounded by anybody I felt cared about me. My pride said I didn't need anyone, but I did. I had to build up the courage to speak up for myself. I had to swallow my pride. I had to tell people I needed help, and I wanted to go home and be with my wife—the one person I knew cared about me and whom I could trust. I longed to be with my team at work because they knew me, and I could be real with them. And I did it. I talked to the people in charge, saying, "I need help with what I'm going through. I don't feel safe. I don't trust myself. I don't know where I'm at right now. I need to go home."

I got a greenlight. I went home.

When I shared this series of events with my therapist, he assessed the situation in the context of my life and said, "This was probably the first time in your life when you were put in that type of situation and chose to change your defense strategy. Instead of just going into survival mode, putting up a wall and fighting through it, you identified a safe place you could go to, with people who care about you."

At the moment, I discovered something new. With the grace of God, I can influence my outcome; I can manage my time, thoughts, and emotions. I have to make different decisions and change the way I live. I can't control anyone's actions but my own.

In the last few years, I have received a lot of help. Many good men and women have influenced me in positive ways leading to outcomes I am pleased with and proud of. I want to be that sort of influence for others—especially men. Men don't feel comfortable talking about their feelings because they are told they shouldn't. Men are told they must convey strength and power and that expressing emotions and having feelings is the opposite of leading out of strength.

This is where the pressure comes from: not being real, not being honest. People shut down when anxiety, fear, and worry get in the way of life because they are not allowed to experience the raw reality of all of their emotions in a vulnerable way. I've heard the difference between being vulnerable and being authentic is this: vulnerability comes in the moment—when the pain is real and the tears are ready to burst; authenticity is most often revealed when the pain is relegated to the past.

We need more strong men giving other men permission to be vulnerable. We need more women to feel comfortable being vulnerable at work and on social media. Our kids need moms and dads, preachers and teachers, bosses and coaches to be real. This is where we can fight back against hopelessness. When kids say life has no meaning, their heart's cry is: "My life has no meaning!" If all they do is compare their mediocre life to the highlight reel of a person they will never know, depression and suicide will become their best friends. We can be better friends, mentors, youth pastors, bosses, and big brothers and sisters. We must be; people need us to be.

When was the last time you checked on the people closest to you?

I encourage you to think, whom am I avoiding? What hard conversation needs to happen? We are often afraid to delve into the murky waters of relationships because we tell ourselves stories of how things aren't going to end well. If you are like me, you often write the end of the story before you've read the chapter. To that, I say, muster the courage: make that uncomfortable phone call. Life is too short to carry the weight of disappointment, resentment, and hurt. And it's slowing you down from living. You only get one round at life, and tomorrow is not promised.

4. HOW DID YOU GET STARTED AS A CHEF?

Give instruction to a wise man and he will be still wiser;
teach a righteous man, and he will increase in learning.

I got into kitchens out of necessity. I joined a culinary program in high school because it was a guaranteed meal, and I'd probably get the opportunity to meet some girls. At Metro Tech High School, outside of the core curriculum, we could choose a vocational skill to study: auto-shop, carpentry, plumbing, etc. Of the options presented, the only one to offer free food was the culinary program. Listening to the grumble of my stomach and remembering my home economics teacher, Mrs. Kimbrough, saying, "You know, Brother, you are pretty good at cooking. You should consider going to culinary school," I signed up. Thank you, Mrs. Kimbrough!

I never thought about college, much less a career. I planned to join the military; much of my family served in the military. At the end of my junior year, about the same time I was being rejected by a Marine Corp recruiter because of my asthma, one of my classmates in the culinary program was receiving a partial scholarship to attend culinary school.

Curious about how it worked, I asked my instructor, Chef Jim Holman, "Is that something I can do? Can I get a scholarship?"

"How is your grade point average?" he asked.

"My grades are good this year, Chef," I said proudly.

"No, what is your cumulative GPA?" he clarified, shaking his head.

"What do you mean?" I inquired.

"Brother, you have some homework to do," he advised. "Go to your home school and ask them for your cumulative GPA. If you want a chance at a scholarship, you have to have at least a 3.0, plus you'll need to start cooking in a real kitchen."

I walked into the administration building the next morning at Trevor G. Browne High School and hit the silver bell to summon the receptionist.

"Can I get a copy of my cumulative GPA printed out?" I asked softly.

My nerves were already telling me what I was about to read. The receptionist handed me the sheet of paper, and I put my headphones back on as I began to read the summary. Every grade I had made throughout my entire high school career was typed in bold black ink. All those classes I had skipped my freshman year were reflected in the D's and F's for each semester. My sophomore year was no better as I stayed in trouble because of the drugs and alcohol I had become so dependent on. The bottom of the page included my cumulative GPA: 1.9. The only reason it was even that high was that I had been putting in an actual effort throughout my junior year. I loved going to the vocational culinary program, which meant I had to attend the other classes to continue being allowed to participate. My GPA was nowhere near the 3.0 GPA I needed to qualify for any scholarships. It was going to take straight A's my entire senior year just to end up with a 2.0. (If you're reading this and you're currently in high school, please remember every grade you receive at the end of each quarter will be reflected in your senior year when you begin to apply for college scholarships.)

As I walked into the campus foyer, I refused to wallow in my failure. My decision had been made. This half-truth on paper wasn't going to stop me. All this report stated was that I didn't care about my future. It had hit the nail on the head. I hadn't cared about it until recently. It was time to change my narrative and take control of my trajectory. My eighteenth birthday wasn't too far away. I needed to stop blaming other people for my decisions. I told myself: You will be going to culinary school. Forget what they said you couldn't do.

I needed to find a different option to pay for the tuition; it obviously wasn't going to be on my academic merit. But I knew I could depend heavily on my hustling abilities. Culinary school cost about thirty grand back then. I was going to make it happen by any means necessary, even if it required creating my own miracle.

I launched into the summer before my senior year with a fire lit by pride and determination—a function of my ever-present insecurities. I started applying for jobs, riding the bus back and forth throughout Phoenix and Scottsdale to drop off applications. I applied at Tarbell's & Barmouche, Vincent's on Camelback, Michael's at the Citadel, and Mary Elaine's in the Phoenecian. I wanted to work somewhere high-end. It seemed nobody was interested in me or willing to take a chance. The only chef to call me back was Randy Saito from the Hyatt Regency Phoenix.

On all of my applications, I had listed my girlfriend, Tina Turner, as a personal reference. I'm sure Chef Saito was less than enthralled with my experience, but he called anyway.

"Is this Mr. Luck?"

"Yes, sir, it is."

"This is a real person?"

"Yes."

"Do you really know Tina Turner?"

"Yeah, I do, but not the one you are thinking of."

"This is Randy Saito. I'm the executive chef at the Hyatt Regency Phoenix. I have your application in front of me. And I have to say, I thought it was a joke, but human resources tells me you are for real. I mean, you put down Tina Turner as a reference, and your name is Brother Luck. I thought to myself, 'I have to call this guy and find out what the story is.' Can you come in for an interview?"

I met with him the following day for an interview. We sat in his office located in the middle of a busy hotel kitchen. It was the year 2000, and the popular song "Who Let the Dogs Out" blared from the speakers above the nearby pastry shop as Chef Saito bobbed his head to the beat.

The executive chef was extremely nice and approachable. He was nothing close to what I had imagined. We sat and discussed dishes from my current job at Wingers, where I was a line cook. He also was interested in what I had been learning in the culinary program at Metro Tech. I was offered the job. New hire orientation would be only one week later.

After eight hours of training and twiddling pipe cleaner flowers, I walked to the upstairs kitchen to express my gratitude to the chef, which led me to another industry lesson. Shaking his hand, I said, "Thank you, Chef. I won't let you down. Whatever you need, I am your guy."

"Really, what are you doing tonight?"

"What do you need, Chef?"

"We're shorthanded and can use you in the kitchen."

"I'm in, Chef."

"Great! Go grab a chef's coat and head to the fine-dining kitchen."

Having grabbed my coat and taken the elevator to the twenty-fourth floor, I walked into The Compass Room, a revolving top-floor restaurant and rooftop lounge. I was surprised to see a fellow student from my culinary class working in the kitchen.

"This is Joe De La Rosa," Chef Saito gestured as he introduced me to my classmate. I immediately recognized him and could tell from his inquisitive stare he had seen me before as well, but we didn't really know one another.

"Your name is really Brother Luck?" said Joe, smirking as he deep fried capers to a crunch. "Yeah, it's my real name. Don't you go to Metro Tech?" I replied.

"I knew you looked familiar. You'll be working the seafood station with me tonight so keep up and just say 'Yes, Chef!' to everything they ask you," blurted Joe through a hearty laugh while snapping his fingers to convey his command of the kitchen.

I quickly settled into the kitchen and began to help Joe prep the remainder of his list for the busy Friday night we were about to embark on.

- Blanch 1 case of broccolini
- 2 quarts yellow tomato coulis
- 2 quarts red pepper coulis
- 10 each spiralized beets
- 1/9 pan peppercorn crust for tuna
- ⅙ pan cucumber salsa
- 2 sheets of lavash crackers
- 200 each crab cakes
- 2" pan parsnip straw

I was finally in a real kitchen, with real chefs, on my way to discovering my joy in preparing fine food.

Throughout my senior year, I went to school in the morning, studied in the culinary program during the afternoon, and worked in The Compass every night. Day after day, month after month, I was apprenticed by mentors who knew something about me that I did not know—I was worth the hassle.

I was immersed in the culinary industry and became surrounded by white coats and checkered pants. I don't believe anyone knew it yet, but I was beginning to control my narrative and was on my way to becoming a decent cook.

I was having tremendous success in the high school's culinary program. They say luck is what happens when preparation meets opportunity. I was completely ready for the introduction.

I jumped into citywide competitions where students from various high schools would compete against each other. And, as luck would have it, I started winning.

Brother competes in the C-CAP (Careers through Culinary Arts Program) for scholarships against other Arizona high school students. (2000)

I wasn't just learning what I thought I needed to learn; I was learning what my mentors were teaching me. I was soaking it all in. I was busy hustling to stay ahead of everyone else, looking over my shoulder, all the while wondering where I was going. I trained under chefs at school who were preparing me to compete in a regional competition. And I worked at the Hyatt in downtown Phoenix where my bosses in the hotel—both the front and back of the house—were so excited about my competition that they changed menus to feature dishes that utilized the preparation techniques I needed to practice.

Every night I would emulsify dressings by hand, cook steaks to proper temps by the feel of a fingertip, and tourne potatoes until my hands would cramp from the repetition. At seventeen, my work became my practice. Because of their dedication to my success, they spent nine months preparing me for the cooking competitions. And it paid off! I finally started winning opportunities to compete for scholarships.

Richard Grausman, founder and president of Careers through Culinary Arts Program (C-CAP)[1], presented me with an award, saying, "I'm going to give you half the cost of tuition: $15,000 is yours because of what you've exhibited in the competitions and interview. Now, you have to go earn the rest of the money to pay for the other half because your grades aren't quite good enough." I think he could have given me the whole thing, but he chose to honor me as a man and help me discover I could work for it and earn it—I was capable. This was a powerful lesson for me; I was starting to believe I was worth more than the cumulative GPA report I had read almost a year prior. I was beginning to accomplish what I intended for myself—a future.

With their confidence in my back pocket, I went on to compete in my next competition: the Art Institutes Best Teen Chef. After six hours of demonstrating knife skills, poaching chicken breast, mincing parsley, and making a proper *beurre blanc*, I won first place. As the judges placed the gold medal around my

neck, they congratulated me with a certificate. I was named
Arizona's Best Teen Chef in 2001.

Brother Luck winning 2001 Best Teen Chef at Art Institute of Phoenix.

This win launched me onto the national stage for the first
time. I had earned the right to compete against twenty-three
winners from other states. The final competition was in Atlanta.
It was imperative that I was ready for the next level of skill set. We
were going to be tasked with preparing a multi-course meal,
including crab cakes with remoulade, filet mignon with a mush-
room demi-glace and tourne potatoes, and a Caesar salad with a
dressing made from scratch. As the dust settled and the judges'
sheets were tallied, I was awarded fourth place. The first, second,
and third-place winners were awarded full-tuition scholarships to

the schools they were representing. Fourth, fifth, and sixth each received a half-tuition scholarship valued at $15,000. I'd always been good at math, so I knew what I had just accomplished. Counting the C-CAP scholarship I had received earlier in the year, my goal of attending The Art Institute of Phoenix was complete. My life had been hard thus far, but now I could feel the hope for my future.

When I enrolled in classes at the Art Institute of Phoenix and began registration, I pulled the first letter out of my pocket and put it on the table. Bam, here's $15,000! And, and oh wait, what's this? I slapped the next paper on the desk—another $15,000! That was all I needed for the full ride. I had earned two scholarships based on my own merit and abilities.

What's your impossible dream? Why is it impossible? Every morning I embrace the mantra that it's a fresh page, and I get to write a new narrative.

Over the years, many people have asked, "How did you find your passion so early?" I've concluded that it wasn't me discovering my career path as a teenager but something much more powerful. I met positive role models who instilled confidence in me. The positive reinforcement made me crave their attention. I was waiting for words only a father could offer: "I'm proud of you." But that wasn't possible anymore. I thrived on the love my dad gave me. He was my hero. When he was gone, I started to look for anyone who would notice me, care about me, and help me become a man. No, that's too much. I was just looking for someone to help me stay alive.

I finally found what I needed but not necessarily what I was looking for—positive role models who pointed me in the direction I should go, instructing me to do right, and encouraging me to keep learning. I flourished as a result of their care and desire to help me succeed. The affirmation and recognition I was receiving from my role models in the culinary industry were knocking on the walls of self-preservation that I had been building for years. I could hear the knocks, but the walls were impenetrable still. They had to be. Growing up on the streets, I learned: "Never trust anyone." But just because I wouldn't let them in didn't mean I couldn't hear them.

"Well done, Brother!"
"You're really good at that!"
"Have you considered a career in a kitchen?"
"We could use a guy with your skills to help us."
"Nice job."

They measured my success in a way I could not. They affirmed me without comparing me to others. And I liked it! I started striving for recognition from my high school instructors, bosses at work, chefs at the institute, and the judges at the competitions. That was part of my motivation to succeed.

I always was ready to learn. I would emulate those I wanted to be like. And when I got off track, I got hip-checked. Whether I was incorrectly executing a technique or simply growing arrogant, I was put in my place, headed in the right direction once again. (Gotta love structure and discipline when it is delivered with a kind word.)

But for all their blood, sweat, and tears, it was still just words. They might have known how to measure my success as a chef, but they didn't help me measure my identity as a man. Even if they wanted to—and maybe they tried—they couldn't because I wouldn't let them.

I have realized that because of the trauma in my childhood, I have embraced a victim's mentality. This is not the sort of deceitful thinking that says: you'll never win, the deck is stacked against you, and you should take what you can get because the world owes it to you. For me, it is the opposite.

Often, I feel like I don't deserve to win; I don't deserve to be here; I don't deserve to be welcomed; I'm not supposed to be in the room. I have a horrible feeling I am an imposter. It breeds loneliness and hopelessness. I've felt this way on and off throughout my life—notably in Kentucky in 2018.

But for the care of so many people who saw me, trained me, and, do I dare say, loved me, the loneliness and hopelessness would have left me gunned down in a drug deal gone wrong a long time ago.

How many of you carry that imposter syndrome? I've worn mine for years. I still do today. Ask yourself, do you deserve to win? If the answer is no, then why not? Do you deserve to be here? Absolutely you do! There's only one you. That recipe can never be replicated. This is what makes you authentic and original. Your past is a part of who you are, but it's not who you have to become.

5. WILL CHEF BROTHER LUCK PLEASE STAND?

Speak up for those who cannot speak for themselves,
for the rights of all who are destitute. Speak up and judge fairly;
defend the rights of the poor and needy.

How many times had I sat in my room alone as a child struggling with my emotions?

I remember being fifteen years old and wanting to commit suicide because I didn't know how to handle the pain I was struggling with. I had been numbing my pain with violence and drugs since my father passed away just years earlier. I hated my life and wanted to find the quickest exit. I had been conversing with a razor blade for a while but couldn't muster the courage. At the time, my fear of death couldn't overcome my desire to die.

In the coming years, I would continue to struggle with more depressive episodes. I considered driving my car through the guardrail and off a cliff. I imagined the feeling of putting a gun to my head. And one time, as an adult, I tried to find my end at the bottom of a bottle, alone in a Kentucky hotel room.

At the time, I didn't understand why I kept talking to myself about committing suicide. But I did know I should never bring it up in conversation because that information was not safe with anyone. I didn't want to be labeled for what I thought about doing to myself, dismissed for being overly dramatic, or worse, end up in a psych ward.

Being afraid of dying, I learned to embrace the pain. I buried my feelings in the deepest hole of my heart. I hid from people when I couldn't control my emotions. I'd cry, scream, fight, and argue with myself about the pain that was trying to kill me. When I finally wore myself out, I'd put the mask back on and return to an ignorant world.

No one had any idea how broken I was inside. I hated looking in the mirror. I hated certain people and the circumstances of my past. I carried regrets for the kind and loving words I never said and for the people I had physically and emotionally abused.

I lived with a victim's mentality, believing I was undeserving of love or material blessing. The pain of losing my father and the neglect I experienced afterward tore open a wound I could not fix. The emptiness had to be disguised with a confident persona: enter Chef Brother Luck.

I've been on a few cooking shows. Actually, let's clarify that. I've appeared on more than just a few cooking shows. I've run the gamut. I feel like an all-around Olympic athlete when it comes to the competitive cooking circuit.

"Brother Luck, you've been chopped."
"And the winner of the Fourth of July pulled pork slider competition is...Brother Luck!"
"Brother, please pack your knives and go."

These are just a few of the phrases I've heard throughout my cooking career while filming major television shows.

I started cooking competitively when I was a high school student in Phoenix, Arizona. By the time I was sixteen years old, I was winning local culinary competitions. I attended the Art Institute of Phoenix, which boasted the only Certified Master Chef in the state, under whom I studied for two years.

Other instructors recruited me to join their American Culinary Federation competition teams. My ego was out of control. Back then, I felt I was the second coming of renowned chef Thomas Keller.

Brother Luck (age 19) winning gold during the Junior American Culinary Federation competition in Phoenix, AZ. (2002)

I was going to change how people viewed and enjoyed food. One day, people would say the name *Chef Brother Luck* and immediately salivate while remembering the last meal I cooked for them. Statues would be raised across the country to commemorate my contributions to the culinary world. (It's all complete nonsense, but it's how my sixteen-year-old brain worked.)

I went on to become a fairly good cook with solid credentials. I was featured at the James Beard House[1] when I was only twenty-five years old. By twenty-eight, I had achieved the prestigious title of Executive Chef for a high-profile project in Chicago. At thirty, I started my own restaurant in the back of a punk rock bar. Food took me to Japan to study and work in Kaiseki restaurants and to China, where I learned to pinch dumplings with old-world masters. I had been nominated for a James Beard Award in the "Best Chef Mountain Region" category. The television shows were finally calling on me to compete against the best.

Having already beaten Bobby Flay and fared well in my first go-around in Bravo's *Top Chef's* fifteenth season in Colorado, I got an email inviting me to compete on the sixteenth season of *Top Chef* in Kentucky. I leaped at the chance for redemption. I had earned the nickname "Last Chance Kitchen Boogeyman" during season fifteen as I had an epic run against formidable opponents before finally losing against my good friend and *Top Chef* winner, Joe Flamm. *Top Chef* came calling again, this time for season sixteen.

"Why do you even want me back?" I asked the producer who extended the invitation.

"Brother, you were amazing last season and a fan favorite," replied the voice on the other end of the phone.

I didn't believe him. Surely, their preferred chef had bailed or was otherwise unable to attend. My gut feeling was telling me I was simply a last-minute backup plan—my insecurities were becoming more and more of a problem. I felt like I still had something to prove and decided to compete again.

Not becoming the next *Top Chef* in my now-home-state of Colorado quickened the lack of confidence I had buried deep in my soul a long time ago. I thought I had closed and padlocked the door, hiding a spider in my closet, but it had been spinning its web, preparing its trap all along. And my pride was about to break down the door and get me caught up in a web, all alone in a hotel room, surrounded by sleeping pills and bottles of whiskey.

What had happened to me? Why was I so unsure of myself? Where had my teenage ego gone? I was chasing validation and lacked confidence. My head was telling me to go for it. You can prove everyone wrong; if you win this time, everyone will know how good you really are. The pain in my heart kept saying, "Don't do it; you've got nothing to prove." Why was my pride getting in the way of my common sense?

Tina was not supportive of my decision. She had watched how broken I was when I returned home, having heard those audience-entertaining but competitor-demeaning words less than a year before: "Brother, please pack your knives and go." I came home feeling rejected and alone. I had become disconnected from those who cared about me. My emotions were as dark as a bottle of aged balsamic.

Having a chance to prove the naysayers wrong, the people who loved me were telling me not to do it again. "Remember the internet trolls," they said. "Don't forget the character portrayal," they warned. But I went to Kentucky anyway, with the swagger and ignorance of a sixteen-year-old intent on constructing my own statue.

I've talked with many of my colleagues who have competed on these cooking shows; only a few of these contestants have become household names. The reality is you'll get your five minutes of fame, but most likely, that is it. If you are lucky, food writers will reach out and possibly feature your face in their publications. Podcast hosts will discuss your personality and rate your performance. Your social media presence may soar, and you might even get that coveted verified blue checkmark. But that is about all you'll get.

Recently, I had a discussion with a friend who also appeared on a season of *Top Chef*. I felt every word of his pain because I shared the same reality in the aftermath of my five minutes of fame:

"Why don't they like me anymore?"
"Was I not good enough?"
"I worked so hard to get to this point. What do I do now?"

I've learned that five minutes of fame can be followed by five years of agony riddled with loneliness, self-doubt, and mental health struggles. It's great to be the life of the party, the center of attention, the cool kid in school. You get used to the devotion, and the serotonin rush feels amazing!

But just as you are launching your new public relations campaign, your shine fades or, worse, gets tarnished by the haters. The world stops looking at you, undoing all of the validation you once received. I wish I could say I was alone in feeling this way, but a sampling of comments from fellow chefs on the competition scene reveals otherwise.

"My shine has dulled."
"There should be a support group for people who were once on TV and now get no love."
"There's still so much of my story to tell, but no one is listening anymore."
"It's just been crickets. That's how it is, I guess."
"What would happen if I shared how the competitions weren't good for me?"

I hear all their voices. I feel their pain. And to cope, I often build a façade and hope no one will see through it, discovering I am something I am not. I tell myself—and everyone around me—I'm naturally confident. I'm tough. I can handle any situation. I have no emotional attachments. I'm a happy person. I overcome my fear through perseverance. But the reality is I'm not confident. I'm not the tough guy I portray to the world. I'm scared of almost everything. My fear is the biggest bully I know, and he takes my lunch money daily. I'm a mess on the inside and have no idea how to express my emotions.

Almost every voice in the world around me has influenced my beleaguered mind, telling me my identity as a man must be expressed in strength, masculinity, fearlessness, and achievement. I don't recall ever hearing how to deal with my emotions once they were tucked away.

What am I supposed to do with sadness, insecurity, and loneliness? What about my rage and resentment from the pain of my past? Why do I sometimes want to intimidate people by yelling at them? Am I the scared one? And why am I afraid to become the warrior God wants me to be? Maybe it is because I'm just a damaged child still trying to understand what it means to become a man. My pain may run deeper than I imagine, but my hope climbs even higher. Why? Because amidst all the lies, I know the truth about who God has made me to be, and I know I am not alone.

Perhaps the greatest athlete who has ever lived, Michael Phelps is the most decorated Olympian of all time, having won twenty-eight medals. Only fifteen years old when he competed in his first Olympics, he won six gold medals four years later while competing in the 2004 Athens, Greece Olympics (known as the birthplace of the Olympics). Now, nearly twenty years and a total of twenty-three gold medals later, Phelps has turned his attention from the swimming pool to having honest conversations about mental health. He is opening up about his suicidal ideas and his realization that "What I did in the water doesn't define who I am as a person."[2]

Phelps' vulnerability in sharing his demons led to greater transparency among world-class athletes and even the United States Olympic and Paralympic Committee. His courage led him to co-produce and narrate an HBO Sports documentary, "The Weight of Gold," in which numerous Olympians expressed their mental health struggles and the challenges that come from being viewed as the darlings of America. During the interviews, Gracie Gold, an Olympic figure skater, sounded the alarm: "Being an Olympian is advertised as this amazing thing, and they leave out all of the side effects, including eating disorders, depression, anxiety, and suicidal ideation."[3]

Recreation in the form of movies, sports, cooking, painting, or whatever makes you smile is a gift. But we need to understand the risks associated with turning our passions into an entertainment spectacle. How high are the risks? The International Olympic Committee, aware of the challenges athletes face, made mental health resources available during and after the Tokyo 2020 Games. Psychologists and psychiatrists were onsite in the Olympic village, and they created a Mentally Fit Helpline to provide confidential health support.[4] But even with this newfound awareness, it wasn't enough to help famed gymnast Simone Biles. She gracefully bowed out of competition as she struggled with her mental health during the Tokyo Games.

I want you to know every person in the world struggles with pain. Every person has done something, many things, they are ashamed of. Every person seeks to find their place in this world. I promise you this, even though you are never going to find your place of belonging in your work (even if you are a celebrity chef or Olympic gold medalist), you might find something amazing in your family, and you will find your place with God.

Do you want to find help? Are you thinking about having a real conversation with someone that won't judge you? Are you afraid of revisiting the pain you've buried? Me too.

I must plead with you because I want you to learn from my

pain and the tears of millions of others; you are loved, and you are not alone. And if you feel alone, I understand. And there are many others who have walked the same road before you, and they stand ready to help. In the back of the book, in the appendix, I've included a list of a few organizations I've interacted with who serve and care for people just like you me. If you, or people in your life, need help, reach out to one of these groups. They are ready.

And please stop comparing yourself to others. Stop scrolling through social media platforms looking at everyone else's fake highlight reel. Stop trying to get your five minutes of fame. You are worth so much more than the applause from others.

6. CHEFS WERE NOT MY ONLY MENTORS

Train up a child in the way he should go;
even when he is old he will not depart from it.

Having been prematurely released into the world, I was forced to grow up faster than I should have been. Without a dad, I needed a multitude of good people to teach me what I didn't know. Most of my mentors were just the opposite of what I needed in my early teens: they took advantage of me. Growing up on the streets, I learned to commit crimes and threaten people to get what I wanted so I could stay alive and better my situation.

My long-term cynical worldview took shape during my preteen years. Trying to keep my head down to avoid a beatdown, I couldn't help but notice how life seemed to end for everyone around me, no matter how young or old. In my limited understanding as a boy, it looked like there were only three ways to get out of the neighborhood: death, jail, or the military. And between every person's right now and their inevitable end, it was just a fight to survive.

When you are in the city feeling the frightful anticipation of the next fight, you are always on guard. Walking the streets, you have to appear strong—stand tall, broaden your shoulders, strut, and scowl—to ward off the shadows of the hood. I learned from rapper Celly Cell to always be "strapped with my knife," or in my case, carry a sharpened-to-a-point screwdriver.

It's rare for those living in the inner-city or those just surviving on the streets to let their guard down, feel safe, and remember the joy of their youth. There is a constant buzz of fear and heightened awareness of your surroundings that drains you, sucking the life out of you.

Often, when we are stuck in our unhealthy routines, relation-ships, and lifestyles, we just need all the noise to stop for a moment so we can breathe. We need the sirens to fade away, bosses to chill out, and the pressure of the grind to relent for just a little while so we can get a new perspective. We need to look at things differently; learn from different people; reflect on our story: past, present, and future.

It is in these uncommon moments of safety and mental sobriety—when you can breathe without fearing a knife in your back—that you can discover why you started fighting in the first place.

A young Brother Luck (age 14) lost in the streets with no guidance.
(1997)

I found a new perspective on life when I ventured into the culinary world. In joining the culinary program, I was surrounded by healthy discipline and accountability for the first time in my teen years. There were disciplined people from whom I could learn: French chefs, Scottish cooks, Italian *maitre d's*. And I will be forever grateful it came with positive reinforcement—it shaped who I have become.

Not long ago, as I was cleaning the walk-in refrigerator at Four (a.k.a. Four by Brother Luck), I realized I was using a box cutter to trim the cardboard boxes to perfect right angles, and I smiled. In 2001, I worked in a hotel under a *garde manger chef* (a traditionally French title that translates as "keeper of the food"). She was a dedicated professional (if not a little compulsive) who diligently maintained the cleanliness and organization of the kitchen. Every day, she would attend to the walk-in cooler, trimming every edge of every box and arranging them in the most effective way to facilitate the team's comings and goings. At this moment, with my fingers loosely wrapped around the professional-grade box cutter, I caught myself mimicking her behavior. Today, while I am my own man and have become a chef in my own right, I am now teaching the next generation what I learned from those who taught me.

But it wasn't always that way. I grew up surrounded by the inner-city lifestyle and the beat-down mentality that comes with it. When my dad died, he was replaced by older cousins, uncles, drug dealers, street hustlers, pimps, and gangbangers. They were all living the same life I was—stuck somewhere between today and their inevitable death. I learned to emulate them because that was the only way I could survive. That was my perspective. It was the only one I had. And for years, it was the only one that mattered.

The culture around me glorified money, power, and respect. Hip Hop culture is brutally authentic in presenting its view of the world. It was then, and it is now. And in my effort to learn about where I had come from and how I got to this place, I started reading books by street legends whom my black culture identified with, including Robert Beck (aka Iceberg Slim) and Donald Goines. Many black folks who live in big cities feel oppressed. In their minds, they might as well be incarcerated. And most are rooting for a jailbreak. If they can't get out, they want to celebrate others who do. Athletes and rappers are the ones most easily seen, but Iceberg Slim lived large in an era when no black man could become a "respectable" businessman. He may not have been the original underdog, but much of the community rooted for him and was spurred on by him. (That being said, no thirteen-year-old should ever be reading Iceberg Slim.)

Slim was a storyteller who understood the world the way it was, not the way battling races wanted it to be. And he wrote about it in his memoir *Pimp: The Story of My Life.* His life was hard. His mom ripped him away from his dad—the only man Slim had ever loved—to be with a different man. Without a man in his life to shape his days, Slim walked the streets at night, trying to find his way in the world. I saw a lot of myself in Slim and his characters like White Folks. Reading his stories, I learned to view my life through the lens of his footsteps. I was motivated by moving forward because Slim said, "Only a fool trips on what is behind him."[1]

Moving forward was the only way I could survive. And in the mind of a lost teen, scrounging for lunch money, tired of getting beat up, I started to isolate myself emotionally from everyone. If I risked being hurt, I would get beaten; as Slim said, "An emotional debt is hard to square."[2] Like many of those around me, I was watching hustlers and pimps run the hood, all the while inspired by the words of Iceberg Slim. And in some ways, we didn't care if it was right or wrong because it was just the way it was.

We have to set a positive example for the next generation. They are watching us. They need us to point them in the direction they should go. Like every generation before them, they are leery of becoming like us, so we can't insist they become mini versions of us. They are learning. They are craving. And driven by their compulsion to succeed, drive a Benz, live large, and get clicks, likes, and shares, they do what they think they must. They are doing what they see us do.

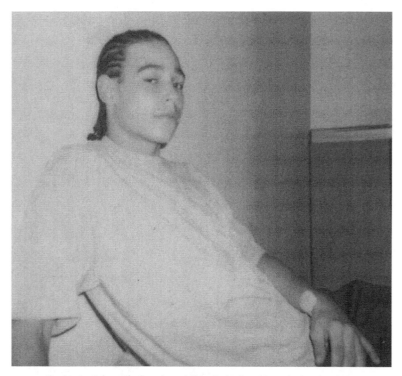

Brother Luck (age 16) after a long shift in the kitchen. Notice his bandaged arm covering the fresh burns. (2000)

When I was a young chef, I yelled and screamed and threw things because that's all I saw happen on the streets and in the kitchens. Fear was respected or, at the very least, followed. I mimicked my mentors until I realized there were other ways to lead, inspire, motivate, and encourage people. Eventually, I gained sufficient knowledge and experience to become comfortable with my leadership style. Taking the good and leaving the bad of previous mentors helped define my identity as a man, chef, and leader.

Designed for community, we will always look up to our dads and moms, older siblings, coaches, and bosses—at least for a little while. We imitate them to become them until we know better. Children, full of innocence, learn to eat and drink, talk and walk, and think and dream by mimicking those who teach them. Good or bad, we become mini-versions of our mentors until we learn, if needed, that there is a better way to live.

As I write this book, there is a lot of pain in this world. I understand it has always been this way, but the pain we are feeling today is our pain. Still, it is good to put things into perspective—I laugh when I read the following:

> The children now love luxury; they have bad manners, contempt for authority; they show disrespect for elders and love chatter in place of exercise. Children are now tyrants, not the servants of their households. They no longer rise when elders enter the room. They contradict their parents, chatter before company, gobble up dainties at the table, cross their legs, and tyrannize their teachers.

Who said that? Dr. Martin Luther King? Dr. Phil? Oprah? Jordan Peterson? It was none other than Socrates, the Greek philosopher. He lived around 470 to 399 BC and is credited as a founder of Western philosophy. Other than the words "chatter" and "dainties," that sounds like it could have been the lament of a Gen Xer or Boomer on any social media platform just yesterday!

Life is hard, but there is hope; and when you're feeling down and out, read proverbs. The American Heritage Dictionary of the English Language defines a proverb as: "A short pithy saying in frequent and widespread use that expresses a basic truth." And truth be told, sometimes they sound like fortune cookies. Or do fortune cookies sometimes sound like proverbs? Regardless, King Solomon wrote hundreds of lyrical masterpieces to guide the people in his kingdom. His wisdom is so profound that it has permeated cultures, shaped education, business, and government, and penetrated hearts for millennia, including mine. Most of the introductory quotes to the chapters of this book are attributed to him, and a list can be found at the end of this book.

King Solomon also said, "There is nothing new under the sun."[3] He was telling us the world keeps spinning on its axis, and no matter how hard we try to succeed in this world, on our own, we are going to fail. And no matter how humanity continues to live, we will ultimately fail if we try to do it on our own without God.

Every generation carries the shortcomings of the former generations because we follow in their footsteps. And we should. We must. We must learn to separate truth from lies, good from bad, and keep what is righteous. I learned a lot from Iceberg Slim, some of it good and some bad. But without the wisdom of King Solomon, my beloved Tina, my fellowship of brothers, and many pastors, I would not know which part of Robert Beck's story I should emulate and which I should eighty-six off the menu.

What life lessons are you following? Whose story inspires you? What do you want out of life? How do you plan on inspiring the next generation? You are currently living a story that can inspire someone else. Learn to embrace that power. Harness it. Your story can be someone's hope.

7. MY ALARM CLOCK

A happy heart makes the face cheerful,
but heartache crushes the spirit.

My independent streak began when I was eleven. When I left school, I'd walk to the bus station, stamp my transit card, and ride the bus until I made it to the BART station so I could go anywhere I wanted. I'd scrounge for money all week to add dollars to my transit card, and on weekends I'd ride the train to the next city and then hop on a shuttle that would drop me off where my cousins lived; I wanted to be around people who felt like they still loved me. The first time I arrived unannounced and unaccompanied, the shock on my aunt's face was evident. I stayed for the weekend, and she took me home on Sunday night and dropped me off in the driveway.

My mother had become a ghost of the person I had known before. The simplicity of just hanging out didn't exist anymore. I felt like she attended to every relationship in her life except her children; my adolescent naiveté prevented me from seeing my childish selfishness. I couldn't see her pain or understand her grief and means of coping. She started filling her grief-stricken void with her boyfriend instead of us; I lost respect for her. Her actions and priorities made me feel like she didn't care about me—why should I care about her? I spent the next decade building walls to protect myself from the world and especially from her.

My mother and her new boyfriend acted like they didn't care about what happened to me or my younger brother, Slade. They had the idea that the streets were tough, and we needed to be hardened by them to survive. Most nights, many of his friends from the neighborhood would use our house to smoke, drink, and gamble. They would shoot dice in the kitchen. They would consume mass quantities of malt liquor and cheap wine. The smoke from all the blunts would cloud the house leaving a skunk smell in every piece of clothing I'd wear to school.

Late in the evening, they would entertain themselves by beating Slade and me. Slade always wanted to be involved in whatever they were doing; he idolized these guys and would hang out until things got aggressive. My little brother was only eight when we started getting beat regularly. There was a routine: they would punch him in the arm, leg, or chest until he cried and then look in my direction and say, "You better step up and help your little brother."

In the beginning, I was scared of these much older and bigger men. Their strength and demeanor frightened my eleven-year-old mind, knowing I would soon be on the receiving end of a similar beating. I'd throw a measly punch, but my scrawny arms and fists failed me. I had no power. I'd kick, scratch, and punch as hard as I could until I was able to save my little brother from the stampede of these grown men beating us up for fun.

As the months progressed, I started to strategize how to defend the two of us. I started hiding various weapons around the house in anticipation of the late-night drunken beatings.

One of the preferred locations to conduct these life lessons was a bedroom where they would shut the lights off and attack us all at once. It was usually the two of us versus four to six of them.

One evening, having stashed an enormous antique clock radio in the room, I immediately dropped to the ground to avoid any punches when the lights shut off. I crawled around on the floor, running my hands against the sandy carpet, scrambling to find the power cord to the clock. The tears streamed down my face as I began to swing the alarm clock around my head and target any large object moving in the darkness. When they started groaning and screaming in pain, I knew the tables had turned. My little arms continued to swing as hard as I could, playing dodgeball in the night.

I dropped the alarm clock and squinted through my rage as the bedroom door swung open, and a burst of light shined into the room. Beads of sweat fell off my face as I collapsed on top of my younger brother, trying to protect him from any more punches. I knew we had won that night's battle and earned some respect, but tomorrow would mean more alcohol and retaliation.

No child should be abused. Ever. But I was. And I was quickly losing my childhood, just like my abusers surely had. These grown men had been raised in the streets, and they were doing what they learned from their "mentors" (I say this in the least respectful way possible and with ridiculous air quotes). Life had stripped them of their dignity and beat them down; it was my turn to run the gauntlet, and I ran it well.

I found pleasure in numbing my pain with drugs and alcohol; I forgot what real love felt like. My emotions had become an ice cube. They were hardened and cold, but I was not strong like a diamond. I could crack under any pressure. The idea of warmth or comfort meant I'd shatter into a million pieces.

As the years passed, I became self-sufficient. To survive the streets, you need to be hardened. You go through a type of boot camp for years. You learn to be tough on the streets by getting beaten up and left bloody in an alley. Your friends help you grow thick skin by hurling vicious and vulgar insults at you day and night. We all know mental training requires discipline, but there is a chasm of difference between discipline and abuse, and I never received discipline from the streets.

A glimpse of a troubled young Brother Luck. (age 15)

The people I was hanging out with taught me how to make a fast buck—robbing people became a game. Stealing purses and wallets is easy when there's a gun involved. Eventually, I was promoted. Selling drugs fueled my habit and supplied me with the money to buy whatever I needed. From the ages of eleven to sixteen, the only rules were those of the streets: learn to mind your own business and never get involved in things that don't concern you; always be aware of your surroundings because things can go from bad to worse in a second; never trust anyone because they will always choose themselves over you; don't let anyone get too close because that's how you will get hurt; and the most important rule of all is to do whatever is necessary to survive the day.

I did what I wanted, and I always had a plan. How would I get out of the consequences if I ever got caught for my actions? My younger brother never thought this way. He was arrested by the time he turned twelve and stayed in and out of jail for most of his teenage years. We are only three years apart, but it was opposite ends of the spectrum with us.

Trouble always seemed to find me. I had gotten involved with the wrong group of people, and it became violent. A close friend was beaten so badly that he ended up in intensive care. I started carrying one of my cousin's nine millimeters; I'd steal his weapon from underneath his mattress in the morning and return it when I got home. (I don't know if he ever noticed it was missing; I was willing to deal with his wrath if he noticed it was gone.) I felt safe when I carried it, and my sharpened screwdriver became my backup. I was a boy to be used and abused by the people who were supposed to be neighborly. Even Mr. Rogers couldn't have shown me a beautiful day in my neighborhood.

My mother couldn't understand my fear when I asked her not to send me to the new school she had just enrolled me in. if I showed my face in the wrong neighborhood, I'd be an enemy target, which wasn't ideal. It's one of the only times I remember her listening to me after my dad died. She moved us to a different city and gave me a chance to start over, but nothing changed. Within a few weeks, I had found a similar type of crowd. I was involved in a lifestyle no child should ever be in. The lesson to be learned was this: relocating will never change who you are. You will always be the same person until you decide you're ready to make a real change.

Throughout all of this, my mother never stopped providing for us. When the social security checks arrived, I assumed they mainly paid the rent because we always had a place to stay, though I didn't spend more than one year in any school until I was a junior in high school. Do you know what it's like to constantly start over? It's like the Bill Murray movie *Groundhog Day*—a repetitive cycle of the same routine over and over unless you change who you are.

I was listening to the music of the streets, reading books about the streets, and acting as if I belonged on the streets. I was emulating everything these older, wiser men were teaching me. Think about it: they were still alive, hadn't joined the military, and most had somehow stayed out of prison—they were beating the odds! I thought to survive, I needed to be just like them.

I was learning I shouldn't have nice things because, if I did, I would have to defend myself when someone came to take them. Nice clothes? No. Jewelry? No. Stereo? No. In my young mind, potentially being a victim of a crime quickly became the same as "I don't deserve nice things." I started to believe a lie about who I was, and there was no one around to teach me the truth.

When a child experiences the trauma of losing a parent, no matter the cause—sickness, violence, broken relationship—all is lost in the child's mind. The scar he or she carries covers the wound of fear and doubt stemming from losing the person supposed to protect you. "My dad can beat up your dad" only works if you have a dad. Losing my dad at such a young age created uncertainty, fear, and doubt. All I could do to feel safe was pretend to be a man. And at ten years old, it wasn't remotely possible.

I tried, but the consequences were grim. I became a very isolated person, which still plagues me today because I didn't want to be taken advantage of. Growing up, I never had a best friend to hang out with on the playground because we were always moving. The move was almost always into a new neighborhood with new streets and new schools—Alameda, Concord, Vallejo, Pittsburgh, Oakland, Prescott, Phoenix. I didn't go to the same school for more than a year until I was a junior in high school.

In my teens, I was an angry kid. I didn't like school. I didn't like the world. I didn't like my life. All I wanted was my hoodie and my headphones. I didn't want to socialize. I found ways to numb the pain. Drugs. Music. Reading. I escaped as often as I could.

I just didn't care. I didn't care about the future. I didn't care about going to school. I didn't care about what I would do once I got through school (or if I even did). It was more interesting to hang out with pimps, prostitutes, drug dealers, and gangbangers. I thought I was learning all I needed to learn from them.

My best friend at thirteen was an aspiring pimp. He was a few years older than me. His front gold tooth would bling in the sunlight—you could see the imprint of his initials engraved into the gold. He would spit game at me: he trained me in the art of storytelling. These were well-rehearsed lies used to manipulate his girls into selling their bodies for his profit.

I latched on to everything he said. I followed him everywhere. I'd watch his girls turn tricks up and down the street. We'd sit and smoke blunts. The cheap brandy kept my head numb. We laughed. He told me what he was going to do with all of his money. I was only thirteen. I was gaining a perspective on life that no classroom could offer.

I soaked up every word thinking he was an Iceberg Slim book come to life. My respect for him was partly admiration but mostly fear. He kept money in my pocket. I felt like I was part of his family.

All that changed one afternoon when one of his girls challenged his authority; she slapped him in public. Watching him beat that poor woman until she was bloody and bruised was a reality check. The cool people I hung around could become dangerous in a split second. My stomach turned as I watched in horror; I was too scared to intervene. He was twice the size of me.

I felt helpless as I watched his Air Jordans kick her unconscious body lying on the sidewalk.

As much as the streets are glamorized in music and pop culture, it's gruesome and sickening, especially when you see it with your own eyes.

Not all mentors are good.

Whom do you consider mentors in your life? What are they teaching you? Are they the right mentors or the wrong ones? For years, I didn't know the difference. Do you?

8. HALFRICAN

Whoever walks with the wise becomes wise,
but the companion of fools will suffer harm.

M ost kids don't feel like they belong when they are the new kid in school, especially when they look different than everyone else and carry a unique name. New school after new school, I would maintain my anonymity for as long as I could, protected by my tightly drawn hoodie and Sony Walkman. It never lasted long enough, often ending during roll call in homeroom when my teacher would ask, "Brother? Brother Luck?" The entire class would turn around and look at me, and I'd be in a fight by lunchtime. I was so angry. If you looked at me wrong, I was ready to put you in your place.

I had been trained (or, more aptly, indoctrinated) by the pimps and OGs to embrace confrontation. I had to be ready for whatever would come. To survive, I stopped caring about what people thought and found solace in my isolation. Losing your emotions makes it easier to hurt others. My survival instincts compelled me to initiate conflict to avoid being the victim.

I have learned our early years nurture our behavior and shape how we interact with people, and our teen years influence our ideology, which defines how we view and interact with the world. I was a confused child; my dad had been gone for years, and my mom was doing all she could to figure out life. No one was telling me who I was. Fewer people were telling me who I should become.

But back in high school, as an angry teenager, I didn't care if I fit in or if anyone noticed me. All I could be was the confused adolescent I was. Isolation and indifference were my best friends and my bodyguards. All I knew was I was alive for now, and I was alone.

And so it is with many kids today. While they still hide under their hoodies, they no longer need to hide behind their music as I did. They now get lost in their cell phones, watching and creating videos, and counting likes and followers in the all-consuming world of (un)social media. The false sense of community the profiteers of corporate media have created is diminishing our capacity to accept ourselves and perpetuating an identity crisis in people of all ages, especially our teens. They have learned to cope with the pain of life by only using their fingers to connect with the world. And they are struggling to find meaning and purpose.

I fear most of us who know better are perpetuating their fear by all too often telling them they are doing it wrong. Instead of helping them, some of us are dismissing them. Instead of being their friend and trusted mentor, we push them toward growing relationships with isolation and indifference. Our kids are struggling, wondering if anyone sees them or cares about them as they are, not for how they could be. (Again, the social media world almost always reminds you of who you aren't and rarely affirms you for who you are.)

Being biracial, I've struggled: my father was a light-skinned black man, and my mother is very white. I've never felt black enough to fit in. Some days I don't feel white enough to join the majority. Even as an adult, despite my success as a chef and business owner, I'm haunted by the fear of not being good enough or not fitting in. I wish I were the only one experiencing an identity crisis, but I am not, as you already know from my conversations with fellow celebrity chefs.

While filming the fifteenth season of *Top Chef* in Denver, I was part of an exciting and eclectic cast. We all knew this, and people took notice. The twitterverse entered the fray when 'soulPhoodie,' an organization that celebrates "Black foodie culture every day in every way," proudly announced to the world via a tweet:

"There are three black chefs excelling on this season of *Top Chef*: Adrienne Cheatham, Tanya Holland, and Chris Scott."[1]

My dear friend and colleague, Chris Scott, was the first to correct this observation by saying, "Don't forget about Brother Luck!" Maybe someone dug a little deeper into the bios of the competitors, but it wasn't long before 'soulPhoodie' corrected their tweet:

"WE STAND CORRECTED, There are FOUR black chefs excelling on this season of *Top Chef*."[2]

I smiled; this recognition transcended my family experience. I finally felt accepted by black culture.

My father was adamant Slade and I understand our heritage and those who came before us, including what they stood for. He would have me compose reports on historical black leaders—people like Thurgood Marshall and Muhammed Ali. We often discussed the civil rights era within our biracial household. One time, after hearing me say the other black kids at school weren't accepting me, he picked me up wearing a neon yellow and blue *dashiki* (a traditional, colorful shirt often worn in West Africa).

I had long dreamed about cooking at the James Beard House; my first time doing so was an honor, but my second time was historic.

James Beard was an American chef who lived from 1903 to 1985. He was deemed the *Dean of American Cookery*. His legacy as a culinary educator, traveler, and celebrity chef set the stage for many people like myself. When he passed away at the age of 81, industry leaders formed the James Beard Foundation and purchased his townhouse in Greenwich Village, New York. The home would become a culinary mecca and a performance stage for generations of chefs to come.

Each year, the foundation and the house host about 200 dinners. Every guest chef who has cooked there has been invited, and in 2018 I received my second invitation: Tanya Holland, Chris Scott, Adrienne Cheatham, and I were selected to host the first James Beard Juneteenth dinner.

June 19, 1865, marks America's second independence day. This was the day 2,000 Union soldiers marched into Texas and declared the remaining 250,000 slaves free by the executive decree of the emancipation proclamation.

Fast forward 153 years later. I'm walking through a busy intersection of Lasalle and Wacker in downtown Chicago as my phone buzzes. It's an alert to join the conference call I have scheduled for an upcoming dinner with some of my fellow *Top Chef* colleagues.

"What's good, my people!" I say into the headset.

"So good. How are you doing?" Tanya replies.

"Where are you at? It sounds busy," Chris chimes in.

"I'm in Chicago and on my way to go see Joe Flamm," I reply.

"You know I love me some Chicago," Adrienne laughs because it's her hometown.

We continue to exchange pleasantries and eventually get

down to business. The time has come to plan the first Juneteenth dinner to be hosted at the James Beard House next month.

"I've got Brown Estate lined up for the wines. They're the first black-owned vineyard out here in Napa," says Tanya.

"That's amazing and beautiful. What an appropriate pairing," I say.

"So who wants to do what? We've got four passed hors d'oeuvres and five plated courses to plan," Chris asks.

"I'd like to do my spoonbread and *uni* dish from the show," Adrienne offered.

"I've got a new Brown Sugar ice cream that would be great for dessert," Tanya replies.

"Well, I guess we're partnering on dessert again, and I'll make a pecan pie," Chris laughs, referring to our second episode of *Top Chef* Colorado.

"I think I want to do oxtails for the main course," I offer to the team.

We composed the remainder of the menu as I strolled along the Chicago River on a beautiful spring day.

With the phone call over, I'm still thinking about Juneteenth— the day, not the menu. I'm excited to cook the food I love but usually stay away from, but despite the invite, a piece of me feels like I don't belong, and I'm not accepted because I don't fit the typical mold of a black man. It's not like I can change who my father was, but as I'm preparing to be included in this momentous event, I'm uneasy about my skin tone.

Landing at John F Kennedy excites me every time. This time I've brought my videographer, Dana Keith[3], along with me as I want to capture this monumental event on film. After collecting our luggage, we head toward Brooklyn. Most of the prep will be done at Chris Scott's restaurant, Butterfunk. Afterward, we will head into the city and set the stage for dinner.

My head slams into the stainless steel hood above the cooking range again. I've forgotten how small this kitchen is: it is not meant for the 6' 2" linebacker frame I carry.

I rub my head as Adrienne laughs and gracefully dances from station to station throughout the compact kitchen. She's making *tuiles* that will garnish her uni spoonbread with caviar. Chris is mentoring as usual. He's brought two young cooks from his restaurant to gain experience from this group of African American chefs. Tanya begins to butcher her salmon that will be paired with a summer bean salad and muffaletta dressing.

I'm making my father's dirty rice recipe. It's a very special dish to me. Before his death, he passed down our family's recipe for my fifth-grade elementary project. I plan to turn them into arancinis, a small breaded rice croquette that resembles a little orange (the literal translation in Italian). As the final pieces are falling into place before our dinner service, we gather the entire staff to discuss the menu.

Juneteenth Celebration Menu

Hors d'oeuvres

Red Velvet Macarons with Foie Gras Mousse
Dirty Rice Arancini with Pimento Cheese
Andouille Sausage–Gruyère Gougères
Hoecakes with Barbecued Pulled Pork
Harlem Blue 1658 Ale American Wheat Ale
Anna de Codorníu Blanc de Blancs Brut Reserva NV
Nimble Vineyards Rosé 2017

Dinner

Uni Spoonbread with Calvisius Caviar and Buttermilk Dashi
Mulderbosch Sauvignon Blanc 2016

Nana Browne's Scrapple with Cornbread,
Okra Chowchow, and Peanut Sabayon
Brown Estate 2016 Beteljeuse Napa

Slow-Roasted Skuna Bay Salmon
with Summer Bean Salad and Muffaletta Dressing
Brown Estate Chaos Theory 2015

Braised Oxtails with Brown Butter Grits,
Soft Egg, and Pickled Rainbow Chard Salad
Nimble Vineyards Nimble Hog 2014
Theopolis Vineyards Petite Syrah 2015

Dessert

Deconstructed Pecan Pie with Housemade Apple Jam,
Cornmeal Cookies, and Humphry Slocombe
with Tanya's Brown Sugar Ice Cream
Diplomático Reserva Exclusiva Rum

I smack my head once again on the hood. I'm squeezing
between three cooks as I reach for my grits now simmering on the
back burner of the range. The high flame burns off the hair on my
arm. I relish in the pain of my bruised skull and fresh burn. Now
we're cooking. As Tanya is finishing the plated service of her
salmon dish, I'm organizing all of my components in preparation
for plating.

It's extremely hot, and I'm sweating in places we shouldn't
discuss. There are way too many people in this tiny kitchen. The
flash from the camera blinds me as I try not to scorch my grits.

Thank goodness the sous vide eggs are sitting perfectly right at
63 degrees. I'll have to thank Chris for the clutch circulator he
brought.

The oxtail was braised for twelve hours. It fell off the bones when I took it out of the oven. It's really sexy. Only real cooks understand how food can be sexy. I take a small bite. Damn, that's succulent! To enhance the dish, I blanched Swiss chard leaves. I pickled the stems to add acidity and crunch, and I wrapped the leaves around small bundles of tender oxtail resembling Greek-style dolma. After reducing my braising liquid, I simmer it until it reaches a satin-like texture. I finish the sauce with a dollop of French butter, and there's that mirror finish I was looking for.

I've got about five minutes until they're ready for my dish. Am I ready?

As our last dessert walks out to be presented to the final guest seated in one of the multiple dining rooms of the James Beard House, we all toast a glass of champagne and share a bump of caviar. And we smile as the camera flashes because we know what a historic moment tonight is.

A handful of chefs gather in celebration of the first Juneteenth dinner at the historic James Beard House in New York City. Top Chefs: Tanya Holland, Chris Scott, Adrienne Cheatham, and Brother Luck all prepared an amazing meal with this culinary team. (2018) Clay Williams

We're all beaming with pride. Every dish was a tribute to our heritage. We tapped into our souls for this one. Big mammas were channeled. Our forefathers would be proud. We've done well by all of them.

Today, I proudly embrace my black heritage. It is an important part of who I am, and it shapes how I view the world. I'm not as confused as I once was; my God-given identity grows more apparent with every sunrise. But I know the "Blacked Owned Business" stickers that grace the front doors of each of my restaurants cause people to wonder, "Do you think Brother has a business partner?"

How about you? Are you not dark enough? Do you not speak the language of your people? Have you been called an imposter because you either don't fit a specific mold or feel like a stereotype of your heritage? Do you think you have to act a certain way because of your financial situation, where you live, or who your family is? Trust me; you are not alone.

9. WHAT'S LOVE GOT TO DO
WITH IT

Love and faithfulness keep a king safe;
through love his throne is made secure.

In 1997 we left the Bay Area for Arizona: first to Prescott (for a longer than normal eighteen-month stint) and then to Phoenix. I started showing up to school out of boredom. (When it's 124 degrees outside, it significantly diminishes any neighborhood activity.)

As the summer heat finally relented, I gravitated to West Phoenix, comforted by the familiar stench of gangbanging, pimping, drug selling, and street hustling. My street mentality was too warped to live in a small town like Prescott, and I quickly found the life I had become accustomed to.

It was the same thing in Phoenix as it was in California: new state, new city, same trouble: I once again found the wrong crowd and became one of them.

Somewhere, somehow, by the grace of God, I got out. He started me on a new path where I would soon meet two blessings he intended for me: Tina and cooking.

In most restaurants, a swinging door separates the front of the house from the back of the house, and a window connects the two. One day, while working a shift at Wingers, I heard a voice demanding my attention with a little more sass than curiosity.

"What's taking so long for my food?" she asked, "I mean, it only takes eight minutes to deep fry the chicken wings."

I looked up and took notice of the blonde waitress with hazel eyes. Her eyes connected to mine as I grinned and continued to plate the food for her table.

She continued to draw me in, "What kind of name is Brother Luck? Is that really your name? Do you have a sister named 'Sister?'"

Her laugh made me smile.

Shortly after Brother and Tina started dating. (2001)

Before I could even respond, one of the cooks intervened. "You know her last name is Turner, right?"

I glanced at her name tag, smirked, and laughed out loud. Probably a bit more than I should have: it read *Tina*.

"Tina Turner, huh? So what's love got to do with it?" I retorted.

She didn't understand why I was smirking. She couldn't have, but I'd eventually tell her that my father was a huge Tina Turner fan. He loved everything about the female rock artist and made sure my brother, Slade, and I loved her music too.

As Tina continued to berate me for my laugh, I got lost in a memory of my father and his love of Tina Turner.

Just a few months before my dad died, I joined him in our former living room now-turned fitness gym filled with all types of heavy-weights and barbells. He was a strong man and regularly worked out to house-shaking music. His record collection dated back to the fifties, and he would always find the perfect songs for proper motivation.

Being my father's son, I emulated him: I had my own workout gloves. I cut the sleeves off my T-shirt just like he did. As he pressed iron plate-laden barbells toward the ceiling, I would impersonate him by lifting a broomstick over my head.

One day, in the middle of a workout, my father grinned as he pulled the Tina Turner vinyl record out of its cardboard sleeve. Sounds of "Proud Mary" flooded the room when the needle touched the disc on the turntable. He swayed back and forth in sync with the musical intro and burst onto stage singing, "We're gonna do it nice and rough." He grabbed a black wig that had been laid out for my Halloween costume and put it on his head and did his best Tina Turner impersonation. My father was a true enter-tainer, and his impression of her was pretty good. He shook his legs and rolled his hips to the rhythm of the song. I sat on the weight bench, laughing and attempting to sing like him. With the song over, we moved on to the next one, and without taking off the wig, my dad and I finished our workout.

Many years later, I was quickly enamored when this strong, beautiful blonde waitress came into my life and said, "Hi, I'm Tina Turner." I knew my father was sending me a sign.

On my new path in Phoenix, I was still struggling: my school and work lives were not jiving well with my home life. I spent my days trying to earn college scholarships and meeting with a career placement counselor. I was applying to upscale restaurants because I wanted to learn, grow, and be successful. And then, weary-eyed, I stayed up late reviewing the notes from my night-time hospitality classes.

Tina and I had started dating. She would come over to my house after work and hang out. We'd drink beers and talk about our lives. My world didn't scare her, and she related to my dysfunction. The norm in my house usually included guns on the table, bags of weed nearby, and more alcohol than in a liquor store.

She was a year older than me and had just graduated high school. I was captivated by her tenacity and courage. Tina wanted something different in life, and she was the first person I had met in a long time who talked about the future like it was a real thing. She worked hard and played harder. I instantly fell head over heels for her. Our summer fling bloomed into a real relationship. Tina came from a tough neighborhood in Maryvale and didn't show fear. I figured I'd take it to the next level. I introduced her to my mom.

My mom wasn't a fan. I don't know if it was her fear of losing her oldest son to a woman, the fear of being replaced, or something else, but she didn't hide her feelings with me. As Tina and I grew closer, my mother and I fell further apart. By my senior year in high school, I had pretty much moved out. I still had a room at her house, but it wasn't my home anymore.

I moved into Tina's house when I was seventeen. Having a more suitable environment to live in, I practiced my knife skills, made chicken stock, and practiced various cooking techniques in their kitchen, all while helping prepare dinners for the family. I chose to take a risk and trust Tina, and her love and encouragement helped me get my first job at a high-end restaurant at the Hyatt Phoenix.

Brother and Tina posing for his high school prom in Phoenix, AZ. (2001)

At a time when I had lost any real connection to my mom and brother, my dad was gone, and people only saw me as someone they could get something from, Tina and her family brought me in. They embraced me and helped me understand the blessing of

belonging to a family. By taking a risk on me and, more importantly, loving me, Tina started to soften my hardened outer edge,
wear down my anger, and help me be a good person instead of the
street-life stereotype I had become. She helped me realize I did
not have to continue becoming my past.

Tina and I got married when I was nineteen years old. And
while I was working as much as I could to earn the right to be
married to her, she went to church seeking God's help in being
married to me. Growing more and more aware of who God is,
Tina decided to get baptized to publicly declare she was following
Jesus and commemorate she belonged to him. Being supportive of
her, I, too, was occasionally going to church. But, candidly, I
wasn't going to church. I was going, with my wife, to the church
she was going to. There is a difference. I was there for her, not for
me, but it started to reintroduce me to a spiritual side I had as a
small boy—one I lost when the world forced me to grow up too
fast.

I'm not sure what my life would look like if I had continued
shooting dice in my kitchen, but I am glad I didn't. Twenty years
later, Tina and I have been married for more than half of our lives.
There are no new stories on this journey we are living. We know,
trust, and love each other. And by the grace of God, we walk in
confidence together. There was nothing lucky about our first
meeting at Wingers. And I'm sure glad my dad loved Tina Turner;
I know he would have loved this one too!

I often reflect on this season of my life as I mentor high-school
and college-age people. Inevitably, I tell them you are indeed the
company you keep. You will become a version of those you spend
time with. You will succumb to the environment you live in. Peer
pressure, negative or positive, is a force to be reckoned with. And
when you realize you are in a situation that is not supportive of
you and your goals, you have to get out as quickly as possible. I
am grateful I had someone help me do exactly that. Tina saw my
potential. She saw something in me I didn't see in myself.

Do you keep telling yourself that you don't deserve love? Are your insecurities building walls? I personally didn't know love until I made the decision to let it in. If Tina is the hero in my story, who's yours? If you haven't met them yet, it's never too late. I'm my own worst enemy most of the time. Joy is often found when you have someone to share your ups and downs with.

10. CALIFORNIA SUNSET

Do not crave his delicacies for that food is deceptive.

S till young but not as hopeless, I chose to live differently than before. While the lies of my pre-teen and teen years still haunted me, they were not as loud and menacing as they once were. From Metro Tech and Wingers to the Hyatt and Mr. and Mrs. Turner, I had people I wanted to make proud of me. With their commitment and encouragement, my teachers, bosses, and new family became more important to me. They were accepting, coaching, and inspiring me, and I wanted to say thank you by becoming the person they told me I could be.

All my professional success, especially in the earliest moments of my career, is attributable to their affection for me. Yes, I worked for it, fought for it, and earned it but always with the support of people who knew me, walked the road in front of me, looked back at me, and helped me find my way.

After finishing high school, I jumped full force into kitchens and hospitality. When I was only nineteen years old, I was offered a management position (outlet sous chef) overseeing three different restaurants in a seven-hundred-room hotel with a staff of more than thirty people.

I carried myself as a much older and more mature person. I had to grow up far earlier than I should have. I was still a kid, but I had lived more of an adult life and experienced more pain and hardship than some people will experience in their entire lives.

When you're thirteen years old trying to figure out where your next meal is coming from, your hunger pains birth distrust, distrust breeds skepticism, and skepticism, if unchecked, gives way to cynicism. I was cynical; sometimes, I still am. I had been a loner for so long; my old ways wouldn't let go even as I tried to hide them in the past.

I had been there before; I knew the way back, but I didn't want to return. Now, in the first few years of my career in culinary, far removed from the streets of the Bay Area, I struggled to separate my identity from my memories.

Surrounded by people whose respect I had earned, I kept feeling like I didn't belong, I wasn't worthy, and I was living a lie. It was easy for me to distrust people, even those who trusted me. By the time I was twenty years old, I had spent half my life trying to stay safe. And if it is people you need to protect yourself from, you quickly learn the safest thing you can do is avoid people— emotionally, physically, spiritually.

Having escaped the streets and made something of myself in the culinary world, I wanted more. I didn't want to go back to what I was. I still did not know whom I was becoming, but I knew I didn't have to become my past. I continued looking for opportunities to grow professionally and keep the fear of being an imposter at bay. So when the invitation came to return to California, not for good but to work with and learn from some of the world's best chefs at a food and wine event, I jumped at the chance.

One of our sister properties, the Park Hyatt Carmel, was catering a wine-tasting for 1,000 guests at the Chalone Vineyard in Salinas. The Hyatt Phoenix Regency tasked two of us, Tony Bones, our banquet sous chef, and me, to participate in the event. I was so excited; this would be my first time returning home to California since I escaped the trouble of my past. I was going, not as a troubled street kid but as a professional chef.

Tony and I had worked together for two years and developed mutual respect. He was twice my age. I learned a lot from him—professionally and personally. Though pragmatic and humble, he loved luxury. Most importantly, he was a man who could be trusted. Tony was the first grown man to ever share his trust with me: he was the first man who ever talked to me about his struggles with mental health. I'm grateful he trusted me and, by simply listening, I was able to affirm him.

Looking back on our time together, I realize his vulnerability showed me I was not alone in my struggles. His story influenced my life. I don't know if I considered him my mentor, but I am proud to say I have become like him, sharing my life and my story with others who need to know they are not alone.

My reintroduction to California was an awakening. Tony rented a fully-loaded Audi at the airport, and we toured the beauty of the California Coast and wine country in style. My room wasn't quite ready when we arrived at the hotel, so the front desk clerk upgraded me to a private condo. I couldn't believe my eyes when I opened the door. There was a hot tub in the living room. The two floors echoed Robin Leach's catchphrase: "This is the lifestyles of the rich and famous."

The hotel was situated on the Pacific coast's edge. Every window offered a breathtaking view. The scent of saltwater flooded my nostrils as I opened the patio doors and stepped onto the balcony.

I watched the cold water waves repeatedly crash onto the rocks below before, and the nearby binoculars soon became my eyes as I scanned the ocean, searching for whales and sea lions.

The view of the Pacific Ocean from Brother's hotel room at the Park Hyatt Carmel. (2003)

In awe of the moment and the nostalgia it came with, I was transported back to Pier 39 in San Francisco. I remembered my mom handing me money to pay for the coin-operated binoculars. As a kid, I would always peer through the lens, searching for sea life and studying Alcatraz.

This was the first time I had ever been on a work-related trip, and I was traveling in style. Tony and I had spent the last few years cooking in restaurants serving many wealthy diners, and now I was on the other side of the table, enjoying a new taste of life.

My welcome note sat atop a fruit and cheese amenity. It stated I was allowed to order one meal per day from room service. After scanning the menu, I ordered a Kobe beef burger and black truffle French fries. I sat in my ocean view room and chuckled as the fat dribbled down my hands. I savored every bite, soaking it all in. This is what it feels like to "make it." I called Tina and described every detail. Not wanting to forget the moment, my disposable camera quickly filled up.

Over the next few days, I'd continue to taste some of the

highest quality ingredients I'd ever seen in my cooking career: fresh black truffles, grade A foie gras, fruits and vegetables harvested from nearby soil, French red wines that would make even a master sommelier blush. It was surreal. But even more than the moment of luxury, I was struck by the realization I was only two hours away from the pimps and hustlers I had grown up with.

Growing up in the San Francisco Bay Area is not the same as living in San Francisco. Big cities are alluring: Phoenix, Chicago, New York, Tokyo, Shanghai, Hong Kong, Los Angeles. I love them all. The nightlife and restaurants are brimming with personality. Their downtowns are bursting with culture and commerce. But the dark secret of all of these big cities is the plight of the urban poor. Within walking distance of the billion-dollar blocks with their million-dollar penthouses are countless ghettos, projects, and row-houses that have never seen brownstone.

There are two faces to pride. There is satisfaction in being loved, loving others, raising a child, opening a business, and the countless ways of making a difference in the world; and there is the vanity that follows a self-absorbed pursuit of success.

This trip to California was my first encounter with luxury, and she was calling my name, whispering sweetness in my ear. The promise of self-fulfillment enticed me. Without Tina back home in Arizona, this trip could have solidified my path toward seeking to glorify myself, my name, and my reputation. Thankfully, it was time to jump on the flight home and back to work.

Sadly, Phoenix no longer could provide what I wanted. I discovered I was worthy of more, personally and professionally. I didn't want to settle for being an exceptional cook; I wanted more. I wanted the opportunity to further my skills and earn the right to cook at the level I had just experienced. The time had come to make a move in my career. The time had come to test my theory: pursuing a career in cooking meant I could work anywhere. Where could I go that would further my skills?

11. GET BUSY LIVING, OR GET BUSY DYING

Above all else, guard your heart,
for everything you do flows from it.

There is a lie in this world that says to succeed we must do it on our own because it is the only way we can claim all the credit for ourselves. And if we want to win in life, we need to follow our dreams at all costs, sacrificing people along the way.

While you need to be you and should be you, you can't succeed while simultaneously isolating yourself emotionally and relationally from everyone in your life. You need people. And people need you. Thinking back to the first few years of work and marriage, I would have benefited from letting a few more people into my life.

Still newly married and wanting to make everyone around me proud, I started making it all about me: my work, my career, my accomplishments, and my wins. I wanted to prove to my family and friends I was worthy. The only way I knew how to do that was by demonstrating my competence and working my ass off. Then it all came crashing down; I was admitted to the hospital with double pneumonia just before my twenty-first birthday. I spent two weeks in a hospital bed fighting for my life.

I had been taught chefs don't get sick, and we need to be unbreakable. I wasn't bothered by sacrificing my health in favor of doing my job. During one of the busiest months at the hotel, I developed a cough that quickly turned to a fever with body aches. I continued to work through the pain, telling myself the kitchen needed me. One morning while getting ready for work, I began to vomit and shake. I was burning up, and Tina demanded she take me to the nearest urgent care facility. Immediately after taking my temperature, they called an ambulance and rushed me to the emergency room. My asthma wasn't allowing me to breathe and the thermometer read 103 degrees.

Hospitality is as rigorous as it is gratifying. Those of us who work in the industry do so because we love the people, like the work, and cherish the comaradery built by the battle. There is so much joy in the wins we often ignore the losses. And there is this subtle, seemingly noble whisper that tells us sacrificing for others is a good thing and we should work more hours because vacation days are an inconvenience to the guest. Besides, you'll get all the sleep you need when you are dead. Laying on a hospital bed while fighting for my life, I learned if you believe this superficial truth, you will start dying a little bit each day—figuratively and literally.

To avoid becoming who I had been—a helpless child growing up on the streets—I embraced the idea of America's long-standing (but currently changing) corporate work ethic: work until you can't work anymore and then just keep working. I have, in recent years, learned work truly is noble. But twenty years ago, I worshiped work because of what it gave me: authority, power, and influence. I commanded respect, not because of the white coat but because of my work. Work gave me an identity. It made me a man. I earned a paycheck, which became my security. And it gave me a worn-out, run-down mind and body that ended up laying nearly lifeless on a gurney.

But God. Isn't that a fascinating phrase? But God, in the middle of a grueling fourteen-day fight for my life, woke me up to a pastor praying over me. I don't know if he was giving me my last rights, asking God to heal me, or praising God for what he was doing amid my suffering, but God had my attention for the first time since my dad died. I struggled with religion for a long time and was very angry at God. I resented having a parent taken from me, needing to fend for myself, not feeling safe, and not being accepted because of my heritage.

During the last few months, before developing an incessant cough and a deadening pain in my chest, my heart was softening. I had been working most Sundays—hospitality never stops—but when I could make it to church, I went. Sometimes I went just to sit next to Tina, and other times I went intent on learning something. Whatever the reason, I always listened. A small part of me felt like I fit in and didn't have to do or earn anything—I could just be. But a big part of me was still the same little street-worn kid. Leery of love, living on my own, I was constantly afraid it would all come crashing down. Surely, someone would be coming to take what I had been working so hard for.

Surrounded by the sterile setting of an inhospitable hospital room, the bedside phone kept ringing; apparently, there was still work to be done. (As I lay in a bed, it was a reminder of how weak I was.) The new chef from the Hyatt Phoenix kept calling and calling. I like to think it was strictly a concern for my health, but I knew better. Just weeks before the ambulance rushed me to the hospital, I had put in a transfer request, seeking a new challenge in a new city after my experience in Carmel. Tina and I wanted to discover what it would be like to be married, out on our own, discovering a future for ourselves. Now, voicemail after voicemail asked me to call the office. I don't know if they didn't know or didn't care, but half-naked and drugged up, I felt like they just wanted me to fill a roster spot and put out another fire, even while I was dying. Tina finally answered and let them have it: "He's fighting for his life right now. I don't give two shits about an answer to when he will be transferring. Don't call back again."

She was scared. I love how she fights for me when I won't or can't.

But God. For the first time in a long time, desperately clinging to life, wanting to live this new life with my wife, I started to look up and listen. Though I hadn't prayed in a long time, I knew what prayer was. My grandmother used to take us to church. My parents were spiritual. I acknowledged the possibility of some higher power. But God, in my moment of weakness, made sure I understood that, though I hadn't been looking at him for the last ten years, he had been looking at me.

I was scared. I had lost thirty pounds. My lungs were failing. The doctors finally found the right medication, some of which I still need today. Eventually, I was healed, left the hospital, accepted a transfer with the Hyatt, and Tina and I moved to San Antonio, Texas.

After being released from the hospital following a fourteen-day battle with pneumonia, Brother takes it easy while visiting with Tina's family. He had to sit down because of how weak he still was. (2005)

Still scared, I was curious about my new relationship with God. I had great expectations of him; I just didn't know how long it would take for him to meet them.

How many of you are working yourselves to death? I mean figuratively and literally. Are you working to live or living to work? It's easy to get caught up in the routine and realize you've missed twenty years. Don't make the same mistakes I did and sacrifice everything for your career. Especially yourself. And if you want to feel noble, just know you cannot take care of anyone if you're not taking care of yourself.

12. DEEP IN THE HEART OF TEXAS

To do what is right and just is
more acceptable to the Lord than sacrifice.

In the spring of 2005, I agreed to a transfer to become the chef de cuisine at the Hyatt Hill Country Resort in San Antonio, Texas. I wanted to work at a resort that focused more on the guest and culinary experience rather than the downtown convention business I had been a part of in Phoenix. Tina and I packed everything we had and drove east, leaving friends and family behind, to start a whole new life in San Antonio.

The move to Texas was promising. It was a salaried position with lots of perks. My role was to be in charge of a restaurant called The Springhouse Café. I relished the chance to work at a different property and learn a different style of hospitality—and Texas is a whole lot different if it is nothing else.

I worked nonstop for eighteen months. I didn't flinch at the sixteen-hour days. Why? It was what I had been taught to do. I was the youngest member of the culinary team and felt like I had to prove myself. Once again, in spite of the sacrifice, it didn't matter how it affected me or Tina.

We had left our families in Arizona, had no support system, made no real friends, and all I did was work. Ashamedly, I'm not even aware of what she did most days while I was at work. I started feeling the weight of my choices.

A little angry about life, and more than confused by how I could be succeeding and failing so astonishingly at the same time, I was wallowing in shame and resentment. I knew it was my fault, but life just seemed to keep standing in my way. A man can only persevere for so long on his own before he gives up.

Young managers often have the positional authority—a title and maybe an office—they need to make decisions, but they have to work side-by-side with the team to earn the personal authority it takes to lead the effort well. The problem was, these chefs were outstanding: I couldn't outwork them! I tried to be the first to arrive and the last to leave, but I couldn't beat all of them.

So I worked as hard as I could for as long as I could. I wanted to learn from these talented people who were simultaneously my colleagues and mentors. I learned best by doing so. Those who can, do; those who cannot need to get out of the way, right? Bad habits are hard to break. How many of us live so we can work instead of working so we can live?

Even though this same routine, only a few months ago, had put me in the hospital, I still didn't have my priorities straight. I was young, married for just a couple of years, and I had no idea how to be a husband. I had made a commitment on my wedding day that I honestly did not comprehend. How could I? I didn't have any examples of healthy marriages. I had no idea how to be a spiritual leader or life partner.

All I knew was if I worked, I provided; and providing for your family is a good thing. I worked as hard as I could to keep my job, earn the next raise, and get a big promotion. I was providing, and damn if I wasn't good at it!

I was so caught up in shaping my identity at work that I wasn't paying attention to anything outside the kitchen. While in The

Springhouse Cafe, I was consumed by the busyness of serving 2,000 covers a day. Every day required managing room service orders, ensuring the success of multiple banquets, and running the busiest restaurant I had ever worked in. My desire to become a chef helped me ignore the pain I was experiencing physically and mentally.

After a full season of Springhouse Cafe survival, the executive sous chef, Martin Pfefferkorn, finally recognized my passion and abilities. He told me that I had earned the right to lead the kitchen for the The Antlers Lodge. It was the resort's fine-dining restaurant and I was honored.

The respect I had for his opinion as a mentor and chef meant a lot. With the upcoming season fast approaching, I was given the task of becoming the chef. All my attention turned to preparing local Texas fare focused on wild game.

Chef Brother Luck plating one of his iconic dishes, Tempura Jalapeno Poppers.
(2017) Dana Keith

My time in the Antlers Lodge sparked the beginning of my creativity as a chef. I began to find inspiration everywhere. Wild herbs and flowers that grew rampant outside giant windmills became garnishes for my food. The oak which burned in the resorts fireplaces were also infused onto the meats of my smoker. Cowboy hats and hay rides inspired me to make dishes like rattlesnake tamales, tempura jalapeño poppers, and hay smoked chicken. Every morning I'd begin the day by fabricating meat. It was the perfect form of meditation to mentally prepare for my long days of culinary immersion.

My butcher list usually looked like this:

- Clean 20# Elk Legs, silverskin removed, 2 oz steaks
- Lamb Lollipops 48 ea, frenched and twine
- Wild Boar Sausage, stuff and smoke 40 links
- Breakdown 24 pheasants
- 6 oz Buffalo Filets, twine and marinade, 48 ea
- Cure and Smoke 4 ea Pork Bellies
- Bone Quail and Stuff with Quinoa, 24 ea

I was finally finding freedom in my cooking. The team I led was young, enthusiastic, and passionate. They had a desire to learn everything I knew. The problem. I was learning on the job as I went along. Every morning, I came in hours earlier than my team to work alone. I needed the time by myself to research and make mistakes. I'd work on various techniques until I figured them out. When my cooks arrived in the afternoon for their shifts, I'd teach them what I learnt that morning. I made it seem as if I had been doing it for years. Fake it until you make it, right? I was such a young chef. I didn't know much. If I was going to continue being the teacher, I would need to further my own education. I made a decision. It was time to go study under some masters. I requested vacation time and purchased a plane ticket back to Carmel, California. Over the next week, my intention was cooking as the student.

I previously had worked an event at the Chalone Vineyard with the Highlands Inn Park Hyatt, and Chef Mark Ayers invited me to return for another. The event? The twentieth anniversary of the Masters of Food and Wine. Many celebrity chefs would be in attendance: Gordon Ramsay, Daniel Boulud, Cat Cora, Roy Yamaguchi, Alain Passard, David Kinch, Ming Sai, Emily Luchetti, Sherry Yard, William Bradley, Dieter Meuller. The list went on and on. But there was only one chef on the list who intrigued me: Marcus Samuelsson of New York City's famed restaurant Aquavit. At the time, there weren't many black chefs cooking on a Michelin level as Chef Samuelsson was, and I was determined to work with him.

Daniel Boulud and Brother Luck pose at the 20th anniversary of the Masters of Food and Wine Celebration in Carmel, CA. (2006)

A Michelin star is the coveted badge of honor in the restaurant world. Initially a marketing strategy of the French tire company Michelin, the stars are now considered a hallmark of fine dining and are included in the regularly published *Michelin Guide*. The three-tier rankings hierarchy is summarized as One Star: A very good restaurant in its category; Two Stars: Excellent cooking, worth the detour; and Three Stars: Exceptional cuisine, worth a special journey.

The opportunity to learn from Chef Marcus Samuelsson was worth the special journey; he was the only chef on that esteemed list whom I identified with. I didn't know much about his personal story. (Of course, I thought it was odd he was running a Swedish restaurant, but what did it matter?) He was at the top, and I needed to meet him. Cooking with Marcus Samuelsson had become a priority on my itinerary to California.

The Masters of Food and Wine was hosted over the course of a week. The experience would eventually become a catalyst for my mentorship style. My first night was assisting Michael Ginor from Hudson Valley Foie Gras.

"Chef, what are we doing tonight?" I asked enthusiastically.

"We're hosting a reception for 250 people and serving foie gras. Any ideas on how I plan on serving it tonight?" he responded.

"No, chef."

"We're going to carve whole roasted lobes of foie gras. Have you ever worked on a prime rib carving station?" asked Michael. He laughed at my confusion.

We served whole roasted foie gras with beet reduction, microgreens, and fleur de sel. The lobes had been seared in a hot pan and finished with shallots, tarragon, garlic, thyme, and port wine.

My week was one memorable moment after another. Chef Mark let me pick which celebrity chef I wanted to assist each day. Every morning I would arrive by 6:00 am. Once the continental breakfast was set, I prepared for the long day by asking myself which chef would I work with.

"Who did you piss off?" one of the chefs said, smiling, as he passed my prep station. I was peeling a mountain of grape tomatoes for Gordon Ramsay. His chef, Marcus Wareing, was compressing watermelon in the cryovac machine.

"After you finish those tomatoes, we need to start working on the consommé," Chef Wareing directed.

We were preparing a rendition of grilled cheese and tomato soup for 250 guests. I stared at the mountain of tomatoes remaining on my prep table. Gordon walked into the kitchen, and everyone went silent. After cordially greeting the other celebrity chefs, he walked over to our station to review his dish.

"Don't stack the tomatoes after you peel them. You'll crush the integrity of them!" Gordon said.

"Yes, Chef," I responded. And to think: I had volunteered to peel all these tomatoes.

Midway through my week, I stood at a prep table with Marcus Samuelsson. He was intense and serious. It felt like he wanted to ensure everyone respected his food and presence. We were cleaning duck tongues, and his sous chef was carefully baking his signature foie gras ganache cake.

"I didn't even know ducks had tongues," I awkwardly initiated the conversation. We pulled the tiny bones out of them while they were still hot.

"The next time you see a duck, look inside their mouth," Marcus joked.

We continued to finish his prep. He was approachable but didn't talk much while in the kitchen. I enjoyed the silence as I watched him stalk station to station. I couldn't believe I was in the same kitchen as him. I had memorized his book *Aquavit: And the New Scandinavian Cuisine*, and I knew the chef would be adding garam masala to the cake batter. As the aroma of the now baking savory cake permeated the kitchen, the chefs picked up their heads with curiosity; I smirked. He was right: the pickled water-melon rind paired perfectly with the cake. (I was studying with a mentor who had no idea I was one of his students.)

Back in Texas, the first thing we did was find a church similar to our one back in Phoenix. On stage and in person, Pastor Soukup would talk to you like a regular guy. He didn't pretend. He wasn't flashy. He just was. And, if he was anything, he was brutally honest. God's tug on me was about to become a shove. As I got to know him, he got into my stuff and challenged me as a man. He said, and I'm paraphrasing our many conversations into one conviction: "Brother, you have to understand you are pushing Tina away. You are working way too much and have too many excuses. Stop chasing validation at work."

I'm not sure I heard him as well as I should have, but I listened as well as I could. Without a male role model, I had found affirmation in the friendship of men who were selling drugs and women. Then I embraced the praise of my teachers and culinary instructors. When the accolades started coming (and real money with it), I craved more and more of what I was getting through work.

Pastor Soukup helped me realize I was chasing validation in my work. For most of us, work is where we are supposed to get recognition for our contribution, receive a merit raise, earn our way to the top, and make sure people know what we did so we can get our pats on the back— this is how the world works. And this is how I lived. While in San Antonio, I am quite sure Tina would say I was more married to the Hyatt than I was to her. I provided for us financially, but that is not the same as being a husband.

Work, for years, had been my house of worship. It became who I was, not what I did. The compulsion to earn what I thought I deserved—the praise of bosses, coworkers, customers, and judges—was undermining my true God-given identity, marriage, mental health, and work. I worshiped my work, and in some sense, I adored myself, or at least the vision of whom I could become. This was the moment when, for the first time, my faith and my family started moving ahead of my food on my list of priorities. Tina and I are grateful our pastor was looking up and listening. That was the moment we started talking for real. We stopped pretending to be married and started living as a married couple. We opened wounds, and God began to heal them.

Brother taking family photos at Garden of the Gods with his wife Tina and in-laws, Chris and Barbara Turner, Joe and Michelle Gungler. (2018) Dana Keith

Something was being awakened in my soul. I remembered years before listening to Kanye West's song "Jesus Walks." If you're not familiar with it, it's brutally honest. I heard it. I felt it. I got stuck in it. Kanye's depth of insight and courage in sharing his experiences—his demons—moved me. Over and over, I heard his words replaying in my mind. I agreed with Kanye; I, too, really was afraid to talk to God because it had been a long, long time.

Young and alone, we discovered we didn't want to figure out life without family and decided to move to Colorado Springs, Colorado, where we could connect with her sister and her family. I had no idea Colorado would quickly become my launching pad for the next decade of culinary growth, traveling the globe, and creating my Chef Brother Luck brand.

In the grand scheme of things, what is our role? The Bible says we are to love God and love our neighbor. That sounds about right. But what does it look like? I believe it starts with humility. Left on our own, each of us will learn to live by ourselves and serve ourselves—just as I did. And here is the rub, or the tension we face each day: We can't live for ourselves. We can't be selfish. We can't live by ourselves. We can't be loners.

As many of you know, I've developed a mindset (if not a mantra) I've communicated often in various ways. #NoLucks-Given. My life is marked by pride, courage, determination, and perseverance. It takes humility to embrace all of these attributes. Pride without humility leads to conceit. Courage without humility leads to arrogance. Determination without humility leads to broken relationships. Perseverance without humility leads to a worn-out, broken-down life. Humility is part of what saves us.

We all need the help of others, and we all need to help others. Do you have the courage to ask for help? Are you determined to love and serve others? Persevere in doing so: you and they are worth it!

13. ROCKY MOUNTAIN HIGH

Listen to advice and accept discipline,
and at the end you will be counted among the wise.

The beauty of being a chef is you can travel anywhere in the world and easily find a job in a kitchen: everyone needs to eat, and there will always be a demand for restaurants. Tina and I put this theory to the test in 2007 when, after seven years with Hyatt Hotels, I quit, giving up my salary, 401k, benefits, and all the security that accompanies good employment. I didn't realize how much I was giving up by being unemployed for the first time since I was sixteen. I would soon learn what John Eldredge meant: "A man needs a much bigger orbit than a woman. He needs a mission, a life purpose, and he needs to know his name. Only then is he fit for a woman, for only then does he have something to invite her into."[1] Tina and I sold what we needed to, packed everything else, and drove to Colorado Springs, Colorado, where her sister, Michelle, and her husband, Joe, welcomed us into their home.

It was a joy to be around family. Our nephews were young, and our nieces were pre-teens; it was completely different from my prior family experiences and a lot of fun. I didn't grow up around a family like this. I didn't know the pleasure of having little kids running around or what it was like to be a role model to children. Sure, I understood employees, and I remembered kids running through the streets, but this was another moment, much like when I moved in with Tina's family back in Phoenix (when I was learning about what family is supposed to look like).

At the same time, the decision to quit my job started to unravel my identity because I was no longer in control of my future. I couldn't come home with a paycheck to prove my love to Tina and remind her I was worthy of her respect. For the first time in our marriage, I didn't have a job, we weren't living in our own apartment, and I wasn't paying our bills.

Tina got a job in the property management industry shortly after moving; it took me a little longer because I was scrutinizing various opportunities. This was a pivotal moment in my career: I wanted a professional challenge, but I also wanted the right fit which would afford me the freedom to become the husband I wanted to be. That's why we moved to Colorado in the first place.

Deciding I wanted to test my skills against the best in the hospitality industry, I pursued an opportunity at the Broadmoor, a Forbes Five-Star and AAA Five-Diamond resort nestled into the foothills in Colorado Springs and I was invited to an interview.

Can you imagine having to audition for your job? While the world has resumes and interviews, the culinary industry has a meet and greet and a stage where you audition to assess your skills. If you want a job working with the best, you have to prove you can become one of the best. Interviewing at the Broadmoor, I cooked for all their chefs, preparing a tasting menu from my repertoire. Humbled and more than relieved I would finally be bringing home a paycheck to help us move into an apartment, I was offered the position.

Before I said yes, I had one more interview, this time at the Cheyenne Mountain Resort—a renowned property with 300 guest rooms, a 2,000-member country club, numerous dining rooms, and event catering. While not a five-star resort like the Broadmoor, the resort was widely recognized and admired.

Following a similar staging, they offered me the executive sous chef position, a much more prestigious position than I anticipated. (Industry insiders and foodies know this is the number two position in the kitchen and the one who leads the charge day to day.)

I scrutinized the competing job offers, wondering what difference I could make. At the Broadmoor, I'd be part of a team full of remarkable talent whose primary goal was to maintain the excellence that defines a five-star resort. At the Cheyenne Mountain Resort, I'd be a part of influencing the future of the company and encouraged to exercise my talents to ensure its success. My mentor, Richard Grausman, urged me to take the position with the Broadmoor; he believed it would further my resume internationally. I felt differently; I chose the Cheyenne Mountain Resort.

From day one, wanting to earn the title they had just trusted me with, I worked as much as I needed to and more. It wasn't long before my enthusiasm and dedication to work once again created tension at home; I wanted to prioritize Tina and my marriage, but I was getting sucked back into what I had always been doing: chasing validation.

For years I had learned to ignore the tension by being all-in on work until my marriage suffered, or by being such an attentive husband, my work began to unravel. I was a pendulum swinging back and forth between two broken relationships. In this season of life, having been challenged by Pastor Soukup, I knew what I wanted to do: be the husband I wanted to be. But if I had been left on my own to figure it out, I am not sure I would have.

Working at the Cheyenne Mountain Resort, I met two people who would become good friends and mentors: General Manager Laura Neumann and Sommelier Steve Kander. Both cared for me and guided me professionally at a time when I needed true mentors to point me in the right direction. In that new phase of my career, I was making the leap from cook to chef. I had been cooking for a long time with the Hyatt and even leading teams— sometimes with members twice my age. But now, this title of executive sous chef at only 23 years old, challenged me to learn to teach cooks how to become chefs. Laura's support was invaluable as I grew. And Steve's understanding of food and wine pairings changed my thinking of the culinary experience.

Brother and Sommelier Steve Kander tasting wines before a dinner service.
(2019) Dana Keith

All of my tutelage under instructors, chefs, and various culinary professionals finally paid off. I immediately implemented small changes in the kitchens that improved profits and enhanced the guest experience. I became a great number two, helping our food and beverage team gain a reputation for high-quality culinary events: we began hosting more weddings, our restaurants started having a wait-list, and our repeat conference business indicated they were coming back because of our people and our food. I was even invited to Manhattan to cook as a guest chef for my first James Beard Foundation dinner.

It wasn't long before Laura, and Bill Poulin, our executive chef, invited me to join the executive team in making high-level organizational decisions. That was the first time I learned about the world in which professional kitchens exist. I learned how to wear a suit, manage people, analyze numbers, and plan the future. They introduced me to all the pieces on the chessboard. My career goal at that point had changed. I wanted to become a hotel executive: my goal was reinforced by an experience while working on a task force at the Hyatt Lake Tahoe in 2004.

I was approached by a man in an Italian suit as I stood in the butcher shop: "Here's my order. Have room service deliver it once you fill it."

I scratched my head in confusion as he walked away; the list he handed me included:

- 2 Bottles Cabernet
- 1 Bottle Chardonnay
- 2 x 8 oz Filet Mignon
- 1 Bunch Asparagus
- 1# Fingerling Potatoes
- 1 Dozen Chocolate Dipped Strawberries

I walked over to the room service manager to inquire what this mysterious list meant.

"That's the general manager. It's his grocery list. He lives in one of the private villas on-site," she informed me.

"Are you serious?" I asked.

"Yeah. It must be nice, right!" she said as she laughed. "You should see the Hummer he drives. I'll take care of the wine, and you grab the rest. We'll run it up to his place."

My mind was blown. I had chosen the wrong table for career day. This man was easily making over six digits, and he most likely had some equity options attached to his salary. Surely, he had an expense account for all his dining on the resort property. I learned he did. And as part of the package, he received a car allowance and a private villa on the north shore of Lake Tahoe. Almost instantly, the idea of becoming a general manager officially surpassed my goal of becoming an executive chef.

The words executive and chef had always been one title to me, but never two worlds. What happens when you place a hyphen between *executive and chef?* Executive–Chef.

These are completely different jobs. They are nothing alike. My high school desires always gravitated toward becoming a chef. Merriam-Webster defines an executive as "having administrative or managerial responsibility." And it defines a chef as a "skilled professional cook."

While working at Cheyenne Mountain Resort, they taught me how to fulfill the role of an executive. Even though I was a skilled cook, my ambitions drove me toward a career path that involved grocery lists and private villas.

Life in Colorado was very good. Tina and I bought a house, developed friendships, joined a church, and enjoyed being married. But at some point, the lies from my past started creeping back in, and my compulsion to move forward began to provoke me.

Continually driven to move as far away from my childhood as possible and to make something of myself, I longed for the next challenge: to become a General Manager.

As luck would have it, the leadership team at Benchmark was launching a partnership with Whirlpool Corporation for a high-end private event center featuring a world-class culinary experience. It was 2010, and Whirlpool was preparing to celebrate its

100th anniversary; this property would become the focal point for a full year of celebrations for the historic brand.

Laura, knowing of my desire to grow and having a love for developing people, put my name in front of the leadership team at Whirlpool.

Having interviewed with various Hyatt properties, the Broadmoor, and most recently, the Cheyenne Mountain Resort—all prestigious in their own right—after four years as the executive sous chef, I was ready for the next step.

But there was something different this time: there was mutual enthusiasm for what looked to become a perfect partnership between Whirlpool and me. The executives, wanting to confirm what they were hearing about me from my Benchmark leadership, flew to Colorado Springs to interview me in person.

I love golf; there is something to be said about the peace that comes from being in nature, the value of learning to manage your emotions, and the discipline that comes from keeping yourself accountable to the rules of the game.

Steve Kander and I packed our clubs onto the golf cart. We had just informed the pro shop we were having a meeting on the golf course.

(When you have the choice of playing nine holes for free or sitting in a boardroom to discuss upcoming business, it's not a difficult decision.) Steve and I were developing a level of trust when it came to our work, and we were quickly becoming friends.

He was the food and beverage manager at the Country Club of Colorado, which was part of the Cheyenne Mountain Resort, and I was the executive sous chef for the entire resort. Even though he was twenty years my senior, we collaborated on every aspect of our operations, and our respective approaches melded well.

Many of our nine-hole meetings involved discussing ways to

enhance the dining experience for our country club members, and it was working. Steve was enamored by the interplay of food and wine and was pursuing his sommelier certifications. Inspired by restaurants like Moto, Alinea, El Bulli, and The Fat Duck, I was pushing the boundaries of my cooking abilities.

So when Whirlpool came to town, Steve and I played nine holes to discuss my upcoming interview.

"What are you thinking about the interview?" Steve asked as he took a few warm-up swings on the tee box.

"I want to do something different. Something they've never experienced before. How do we incorporate the garden that we just built?" I responded as I prepared for another beat-down on the course, courtesy of Steve.

We had just completed a significant improvement to the resort by building an outdoor garden. Having a green thumb, Steve led the charge, and many of the management and their families volunteered to help.

Together we constructed raised garden beds, prepared outdoor seating, and installed fencing to keep the bears out.

The Colorado summer was in full swing; many of the plants were in full bloom, and there was a bounty of ingredients for us to cook with. You've gotta love it when the hard work pays off!

Steve smiled as he hit a straight shot down the middle of the fairway. "I like it. We could do a wine pairing with all of the different herbs we have growing. The curry leaf plant could be interesting."

I stepped up to the tee and hit my shot. The ball sliced to the left, and I cursed. "I want to do a cooking class live in front of them. We can use the herbs and teach them about the pairings as well. I mean, it's exactly what they're hoping this project will be once it's opened."

As we pushed through the remaining holes, we finalized the menu, and I felt ready for the interview.

Whirlpool Tasting Experience

Starter
Chipotle Goat Cheese Stuffed Squash Blossoms
with Coriander Flowers

Entree
Smoked Duck BLT with Tomatoes & Garden Lettuces

Finale
Aebelskivers with Summer Berry Semifreddo

All the creative approaches had paid off. I cooked each course in front of them while describing every technique and explaining how we incorporated the garden into the meal. I had a great time, and so did the executives (it didn't hurt that Steve was a little heavy with his wine pours.) It wasn't long before Tina and I were packing in preparation for our move to Chicago to open the World of Whirlpool, the company's new brand and product experience center: the flagship of their worldwide commercial enterprise.

Challenges are meant to be taken on. You will either succeed or fail. The lesson is in the attempt. What was the last challenge you faced personally? What about professionally? Did you walk away with something? The key part of any challenge is to prepare and to do so with the assistance of others. If you want to go fast, then go alone: if you want to go far, then go with a team.

14. THE MILLION DOLLAR MILE

Folly is a joy to him who lacks sense,
but a man of understanding walks straight ahead.

I had done it. By the age of twenty-seven, I had achieved my goal of becoming an executive chef. My dream of having a great job and an even better marriage seem to be, by God's provision and grace, coming together like the sun and Pacific Ocean.

Tina and I lived in the city and were enthralled by the hustle and bustle of working in downtown Chicago. Every morning there's a rush of footsteps with people on the sidewalks, some hailing cabs and others spilling out of the train stations. And everywhere you look, there are people in business suits with a backpack over their shoulders, carrying their dress shoes for the office. As with every big city, there's an onslaught of traffic: it hums with horns and profanities as cars race from red light to red light. Oh, and I loved the smell of warm chocolate wafting from Blommers Chocolate.

We moved into River North, just off Chicago Avenue and Larrabee. The building was the old Montgomery Ward office building. Our jaws dropped when the apartment broker opened the door to the eighteenth-floor, two-bedroom, two-bath unit. The windows were floor to ceiling and faced Lake Michigan and Wrigley Stadium. The apartment included a dog park for our miniature schnauzer. There were two parking spots in a private garage. (If you've ever lived in any major downtown city, you understand how expensive parking is.) My favorite part was the twenty-four-hour door attendants; they would greet us as we departed and returned.

"Hello, Mr. Luck. How are you doing today?"

I felt like we were George and Wheezy from the Jeffersons: *Moving on up!* We had no business living in a place like this. God has a mysterious way of providing.

We found a great church in Chicago, and we made a point of getting connected with the community there. We also learned how to play. In the summer, we rode our bicycles to North Beach and played in a volleyball league with friends from church. In the winter, we walked to the movie theater and laughed at ourselves while hurling snowballs at each other. We worked hard, loved well, and truly became friends again.

Along with the executive leadership team at Whirlpool, I planned and helped build an entertainment and educational facility that hosted high-profile parties in demonstration kitchens. We created an environment in which people wanted to learn and play. The facility had ten kitchens and outdoor patios with garden beds, fire pits, couches, and shuffleboard.

Rather than relying on individuals and group bookings, we were a destination venue for corporate gatherings and focused on training and continuing education for Whirlpool customers, architects, kitchen designers, strategic partners, and key brand influencers.

We built the event center in a historic Chicago landmark—the Reid-Murdoch Center. Chicago was the perfect city, and the building was the finest venue to create a downtown demonstration kitchen for the industry.

Brother and Tina Luck standing on the rooftop of The World of Whirpool in Chicago, IL. (2010)

Once we opened our doors at Whirlpool, I settled into a Monday through Friday work routine, which was possible because we catered primarily to corporate clients. Having matching work schedules for the first time, Tina and I discovered what it meant to be married—to be husband and wife, friends, and partners.

Just as each of the trips to the Park Hyatt Carmel made me a better chef, so too did my time in Chicago, thanks in part to Perry Kokotis and an evening at the three-Michelin star restaurant Alinea.

Watercress

Perry was intense. His previous experience included multiple stints at Michelin restaurants throughout Chicago. He recently had been working at Vie under Paul Virant. His passion for food compelled me to hire him as my sous chef for the new Whirlpool project.

Perry made me fall back in love with cooking. In his enthusiasm for excellence, he made it his mission to source the best local ingredients for every dish he prepared, and he compiled a list of every farmer from the Midwest region. I can still remember the day a plastic bag of muddy watercress made me forget about the general manager fantasy from Lake Tahoe.

"Hey chef, here's your lamb shoulder on top of everything else you ordered," said the farmer as he brought in the food order for the night's event.

"Wow, these tomatoes are so ripe, and the cantaloupe is wonderfully fragrant," I commented as I sorted through the basket.

"And I found this patch of watercress down by my creek.

Thought you might be interested in it," he interjected as he smiled and handed me a bag of weeds.

Tasting the watercress leaves, I lit up; it was noticeably spicier and more bitter than any watercress I had had before.

I soon learned to value Perry's professional network of local purveyors and adopted them as my own. Order after order, I was a kid at Christmas. The quality of the ingredients reminded me of my two trips to Carmel. In all of my experiences in commercial kitchens thus far, I had never used such perfect elements to create my dishes.

In short order, not only did my culinary standards change in pursuit of an elevated cooking and dining experience, but I also decided to return to my passion for becoming an executive chef. Perry's passionate pursuit of excellence reintroduced me to cooking.

Chefs Perry Kokotis, Brother Luck, and Oliver Malcolm smile and playfully joke before a serious dinner service in the private kitchen at The World of Whirlpool in Chicago, IL. (2010)

Alinea

If you are a serious foodie, you have likely already dined at or plan to visit Alinea, the famed three-Michelin-star restaurant that Grant Achatz calls home.

If you are like me, your imagination enables you to envision the perfect meal on a romantic night with your best friend. Thanks to Tina, who took me out for an amazing birthday celebration, I don't have to use my imagination anymore. Instead of closing my eyes to dream, I close them to remember.

The four-hour culinary immersion consisted of twenty courses, and the execution was flawless. As soon as you walk into Alinea, you realize you are about to embark on a special journey. For more than five years, I had wanted to dine here, and now I finally was.

The entry was a small hallway lined with curtains. The greeting station had only two seats that provided an open view of the kitchen, allowing us a glimpse of the staff composing a symphony of food. The brigade was enormous and yet quiet. All of the cooks were constantly cleaning while working intensely, not wasting a single movement.

After a few moments, we were escorted to the upper floor dining area, where we were quickly seated. The decor was simple, with lots of clean lines, sharp angles, and complementary shapes to accentuate. The tables were illuminated perfectly, creating a spotlight for every course.

We were greeted by a server who shared the story of Alinea and painted a picture for us of what was to unfold in the coming hours: numerous small-plate courses and wine pairings. And with the introductions complete, the waitstaff placed tiny square plates in front of us and topped them with little white pillows for our clean silverware.

Tina's and my excitement grew as the first pour into our wine glasses began, and the team started us on our culinary journey.

The 2011 Summer Menu

STEELHEAD ROE - watermelon, kaffir lime, oxalis
HAMACHI - west indies spices, pineapple, ginger
OYSTER LEAF - mignonette
TAYLOR BAY SCALLOP - hitachino Weizen, old bay
RAZOR CLAM - carrot, soy, daikon
MUSSEL - saffron, chorizo, orange
YUBA - shrimp, miso, togarashi
FARM SALAD - tomato, goat cheese, red onion
MACKEREL - mango, bergamot flower, juniper
WILD MUSHROOMS - pine, sumac, ramp
HOT POTATO - cold potato, black truffle, butter
AGNEAU - sauce choron, pomme de terre noisette
BLACK TRUFFLE - Explosion, Romaine, Parmesan
SQUAB - inspired by Miro
SHORT RIB - Olive, Fermented Garlic, Blackberry
OCTOPUS - eggplant, coriander, red wine
SNOW - yuzu
PEACH - jasmine, basil, balsamic
LEMONGRASS - dragonfruit, basil, finger lime
CHOCOLATE - red pepper, bitter orange, banana

One of my all-time favorite culinary bites was the black truffle explosion: a single ravioli served on a spoon with a slice of black truffle, Parmesan cheese, and romaine lettuce. Following the server's instructions, I ate this course in a single bite and did not open my mouth while savoring its elegance. Biting into the luscious pasta, the explosion of flavor—with the black truffle front and center—sent me into a moment of bliss, one I will always remember.

In recent years, I often have challenged my team members to know where they are going: "How can you become the best if you don't know who the best is?" Because so much of our success is dependent upon following others, we need to know whom to follow. About the same time, Perry was bringing me back to my love of food, I was studying chefs like Grant Achatz. I wanted to learn more about what he did at Alinea and how he did it. As I enjoyed each of these courses, I compared my skills to his. I learned from him and, in some ways, have modeled the mission of my restaurant *Four by Brother Luck* in Colorado Springs after the perfect night I had with Tina. At Four, we *create memorable experiences through food and drink*. I hope that eleven years from now, people are talking about their perfect night at one of my restaurants.

For a brief moment, Tina and I had everything we wanted. But I was being enticed by my first love—cooking. Despite the joys of marriage, friendship, and a rewarding lifestyle in one of the greatest cities in the world, my pride was drawing me toward something that promised to be even better.

While the endeavor with Whirlpool could only be described as a success, I wasn't getting the acclaim and status I craved. There were no food critics writing articles about my new menu. I didn't have a way to host fellow chefs at my tables because we catered to private events. There were no awards to win, no new titles to earn, no restaurant fires to put out. While I held the title of executive chef, all I did was go to work every day and run the business.

Still thinking about our dinner at Alinea, I started looking for a new way to garner respect for my food. It didn't take long before I found my new home back in San Antonio. Yet, it took a long time for me to realize the depth of my sacrifice and the pain that resulted, mostly to Tina.

For those who sacrifice everything to get the title, car, corner office, promotion, or whatever they think will silence the voices or numb the pain, when they get to the top—if they do—their success won't matter because they won't have anyone to share it with. They will have shown their friends they don't matter. They will have struggled to keep their commitments to their family. Their kids won't bother calling because they think they are too busy. Don't believe me? Put down this book for a minute and listen to "Cats In The Cradle" by Harry Chapin. If you know the song, I know you are already crying.

Now, I don't mean to bring up your past or cause you to dwell on your pain, but what have you lost because you chose to sacrifice it on the altar of success?

If you want to succeed, you need to do it with the support of the people you love: the people who love you back. You need to involve your family, friends, and co-workers. And if you are willing to let go of your dreams because you care more about people than your idealism, you're the kind of person I want on my team! If the circumstances are right, maybe I'll join your team!

15. OVER EASY OR SUNNY SIDE UP

Wisdom is found on the lips of the discerning,
but a rod is for the back of one who has no sense.

S till savoring our perfect night at Alinea and anticipating my
next career move, the leadership at Benchmark asked me to
move back to Texas, this time, to lead the team at Hotel Contessa
—an intimate, all-suite hotel on San Antonio's beloved Riverwalk.
After almost two years in Chicago, it was again time. I enthusiastically said, Yes!

Throughout my tenure with the Hyatt and Benchmark Hospitality, I learned to care for people, lead teams, and execute a
variety of high-profile holidays and special events. While with
Whirlpool in Chicago, I gained an awareness of and affection for
locally sourced, farm-raised products that paint the palette at a
different level than the wholesale food-service supply products I
had been using for years. This beautiful property and the fantastic
team at Hotel Contessa had the opportunity to enhance the culinary scene in San Antonio, and I was excited to be a part of it.
Then I found myself arguing about eggs.

As I settled in and learned my way in the organization, establishing my credibility, I wanted to begin the transformation I envisioned when I interviewed for the job. One of the first changes I wanted to implement was to use local, small farm-raised eggs, which were about $0.40 each. Understandably, the financial controller at Hotel Contessa wanted me to use generic, mass-produced eggs, which were about $0.07 each. The show-down began! I realized I wanted to create a more luxurious experience for foodies, but no hotel would ever let me do so. I immediately began brainstorming what my future would look like and set my mind on opening my own restaurant one day soon.

At about the same time, I received an email inviting me to join the casting call for *Top Chef Season 10*. Tina and I agreed I should pursue it. I had enjoyed the challenge of the high school cooking competitions and understood how the exposure could launch my career to new heights.

The invite coincided with Tina receiving a great job offer to work for a company back in Colorado. We made the difficult decision for her to move back to Colorado and live with her sister, Michelle, while I finished the last six months of my contract with Hotel Contessa. With my first big invitation toward the future and Tina's Colorado Springs job offer, the stars were aligning for a bright future.

For the casting call, I was the first one in line at Linger restaurant in Denver, part of the Edible Beats empire founded by Justin Cucci. And I killed it. But in the end, the producer told me, "You've got a great story, a cool name, but we don't showcase hotel chefs." Now, he probably said it differently than that, more diplomatically and more kindly, but that is what I heard.

I was arguing with my employer about eggs, and *Top Chef* told me I wasn't good enough. Tina was living and working in Colorado, and I was working non-stop in San Antonio again. I was driving out as often as I could to see her, but being alone and feeling rejected, I was in a lot of pain. My identity and worth were being undermined by the profession I loved.

During the second go-around in San Antonio, I grew close with Pastor Soukup. He was the one who made me understand it was my responsibility to change my reality. He challenged me to be the spiritual, emotional, and financial leader in my family while trusting God's ultimate love and calling on my life.

For years I had been living under a mantra that looked like jumping off a cliff and building a parachute on the way down. While I had been flying more often than I was crashing, the thrill was not as fulfilling as it once was. Pastor Soukup helped me understand it was time to start climbing mountains instead of jumping off them. Time to ascend to a place of meaning and purpose instead of just circling the base of the mountain, wondering if I would ever get anywhere in life.

Being a soccer fan, Pastor Soukup told me sometimes you have to kick the ball backward to prepare to score a goal. He said I was afraid to do that: I was just dribbling the ball in circles.

I started writing my first business plan for my restaurant in our second-floor San Antonio apartment, which was filled with the scent of my wife, whom I missed dearly. At some point, I realized I was missing some key points in planning a business. How much did insurance cost? What would the utility bill be? How many people could I serve in a day?

A business plan is simply a packet of educated guesses. Banks and investors are often leery because of the countless variables and challenges to opening a successful restaurant. Assessing my strengths and experience, I acknowledged that, while I had an impressive career in large volume hotels (seven years with Hyatt Hotels and six years with Benchmark Hospitality), I didn't have the restaurant experience I needed to risk opening my own establishment. I had to learn how to manage an independent restaurant before I could operate one on my own.

I started dreaming about working in a restaurant that had a reputation for fine dining and a growing legacy. Maybe I could work in a castle or a vineyard? All I knew for sure was I had to leave Texas and get back to Colorado Springs.

Somewhere in the middle of working at the hotel every day and working on my business plan every night, I received a phone call from my good friend and sommelier, Steve Kander. We worked together at the Cheyenne Mountain Resort for four years, he knew me, and I trusted his judgment. So when he suggested I join the team where he was now working, I found my escape hatch.

It was a magical property tucked into the hillside of Manitou Springs, a quaint town with a quirky community just west of Colorado Springs. The giant stone building with a massive kitchen and multiple beautiful dining rooms was built over one hundred years ago by skilled immigrants who created new communities and helped each other build homes. The property boasted towering pine trees; black bears were roaming the woods, and wild raspberries grew rampant.

One of my favorite features of this restaurant was the copper fireplaces encased in stone. The restaurant staff would build blazing fires each night before guests arrived for their dinner reservations to complement the natural beauty of Colorado outside the large glass windows.

I was extremely excited because I had known a few of the past chefs who built the reputation for this place. It had never won a James Beard Award or ever been on a Food and Wine list, but I knew this could be the place where I would achieve those goals. It had everything I wanted in a restaurant.

Tina and I had dinner at the restaurant to discover its current beauty and future potential. I then interviewed for and was quickly appointed to be the new executive chef.

I returned to San Antonio the following day to prepare to move back to Colorado and begin my new life at this amazing family-owned, fine dining restaurant. The team at *Top Chef* would have to take notice. Fueled by my recent rejection at the casting call for the upcoming season of *Top Chef* in Seattle, I wanted to reveal to them the depth of their ignorance.

Sure, my pride was damaged by the individual rejection, but more than any personal offense, the "You're not good enough" was a condemnation of the culinary pedigrees of hotel chefs, who are some of the most versatile cooks in the world. I wanted to prove them wrong.

Running an operation that hosts twenty food and beverage functions simultaneously while exceeding expectations at five on-site restaurants is not for the faint of heart. You must be able to adapt to many situations, care for hundreds of workers, engage with dozens of clients, and keep hot food hot and cold food cold, all while leading the team as they prep for tomorrow's events.

Oh, by the way, you need to go cover the chef on the carving station who keeps asking for a smoke break.

As a hotel chef of thirteen years, I was told (and by extension, all of the chefs I had ever worked with) I wasn't good enough to compete on *Top Chef*—the very show I measured my skill set against. I don't care what any chef tells you; we all want to be on *Top Chef*. Many of us have watched every episode. I've learned tons of new techniques from the competitors who've been on the show over the years. I applied every year and longed for the opportunity to prove myself. The world needed to know my cooking pedigree.

But casting, at that time, wasn't buying what we hotel chefs were selling. They were searching for contestants who came from celebrity-endorsed restaurants: Michelin restaurants. James Beard nominees. Accolades from *Food and Wine* magazine. My soon-to-be success as the executive chef of this historic restaurant was going to be my moment for everyone to notice.

Let's see them doubt my skills now as a fine-dining chef!

Chef Brother Luck entertaining guests at Beaver Creek Food and Wine Festival.
(2018) Dana Keith

I understood my background didn't merit becoming a celebrity chef, but it did merit the opportunity to compete, and therein lies the difference. The producers, at that time, determined that, while I might have been worthy of a world-class culinary competition, I did not deserve the opportunity to become a celebrity. That's the entertainment industry for you. And I really do understand. I had never worked for a Daniel Boulud or a Thomas Keller, didn't own my own restaurant, and wasn't a product of Hyde Park's Culinary Institute of America. But my copy of Thomas Keller's *French Laundry* is tattered from carrying it through numerous world-class kitchens. I learned everything Daniel Boulud wanted to teach me in *Letters to a Young Chef.*

Ready to make the jump from student to teacher, this restaurant would become the place where I would learn the last few pieces to become someone the culinary world would respect. And yes, while it was about proving the world wrong about hotel chefs, I was mostly out to prove them wrong about me.

I finished my contract with Hotel Contessa, sold what I needed to, packed the rest into my car, and drove back home to Tina and Colorado Springs.

16. DREAMS OF A MICHELIN RESTAURANT

Do not wear yourself out to get rich;
do not trust your own cleverness.
Cast but a glance at riches, and they are gone,
for they will surely sprout wings
and fly off to the sky like an eagle.

The restaurant industry relies heavily on this family mentality of camaraderie. Most weeks, we spend more time with each other than with our own families. We sweat. We cry. We Fight. But most importantly, we bond.

Contrary to what most people think, restaurants aren't very profitable. My bookkeeper once asked, "Why are you even in this business?" She doubled down, saying, "You restaurant owners create jobs just to break even if you're lucky."

Most people who work in restaurants do not come from much. Most have limited education; our families are broken, and our childhoods were challenging. And many are immigrants searching for better ways to provide for their families. Many are felons. Some live in halfway houses. Others have been recently paroled. The diversity is vast. It's not a surprise that many of us learn new languages to communicate with each other.

We bond on a different level. Sandwiched between glasses and plates, you will find the people. The burns. The scars. The addictions. The late hours. The glamorous rockstar lifestyle portrayed on television is a farce. It's not a reality. It has never been. Shows like *Top Chef*, *Chopped*, and *Beat Bobby Flay* are created for entertainment. Cooking on television has very little to do with the realities of working in a restaurant. It takes a certain kind of crazy to become one of us.

Commercial kitchens of all stripes are notorious for having hostile work environments, rampant sexual harassment, uninterested employees who are just passing through, poorly trained management, and disconnected owners. I discovered my new home in Manitou Springs was just more of the same. If I wanted to create a world-class restaurant with an environment that honored our guests and employees, I'd have to do it independently.

After relocating to Colorado Springs, we moved into my sister-in-law's basement for a second time. My ego was bruised. I had given up the perks of working in the corporate world. I had never worked for a small family-owned business, but I was ready to change the world (or at least my small slice of it). I thrived on the idea of the challenge: reinventing a restaurant; turning it into a James Beard Award-winning property. (When I look back on it now, I realize how immature and unprepared I was. My skills as a chef did not correlate with operating a restaurant, which requires much more than cooking beautiful food.)

I quickly dove headfirst into my new role as the executive chef. Cleaning would be the priority; they were about to get a rude awakening. I pulled the grill and fryers away from the stainless steel under the ventilation system. I gave each worker a red sanitation bucket and green scrubby. As the degreaser soaked in, I started scrubbing away the months of grease that had built up. My first cook quit within thirty minutes. What had I gotten myself into? This was not becoming the Michelin restaurant I had envisioned during my interview.

Upon taking the helm as Executive Chef of the Craftwood Inn, Brother Luck poses for his first headshot in his new role. (2012)

The plates we worked with were ancient and ugly; they had pink flowers on the rims. The equipment was old; most of it was broken and out of commission. I inherited young, inexperienced cooks who were more interested in partying than learning. My team lacked passion and discipline. These pirates had no desire to follow a captain's orders. A few had substantial potential with untapped talent longed to be nurtured and finessed: the pastry chef gave me the most confidence. She was young but engaged. Her chocolate piping abilities were second to none.

My menu planning benefited from having a massive garden outside the kitchen. I'd spend hours each week harvesting nasturtium leaves, dill flowers, raspberries, cilantro blossoms, pansies, and garlic chives for dinner service. The cooks were not impressed. They were indifferent to the beauty I was gathering from the rich soil.

I prepared an *amuse bouche*—a small morsel sent by the chef at the beginning of a meal meant to excite your palate—every morning, only to find them still sitting on the speed cart at the end of the service as the servers didn't want to put in the effort to deliver them to the tables. Was I the only one who cared about our potential?

We had the beauty. The dining room was perfect. Our wine list was extensive. We were only missing great food, and I was excited to fight to make it happen (as I said, I thrived on the idea of the challenge of reinventing this restaurant).

Eventually, vendors began to demand checks upon delivery. Ownership delayed our payroll for insufficient funds. Manitou Springs had been hit with wildfires. Burnt trees no longer prevented rainfall from cascading down the mountainside. When the rainy season came, the nearby streets flooded, and cars floated away by the dozens. Business was dwindling.

Within six months, there wouldn't be a restaurant. It was the perfect storm. The writing was on the wall. I needed to abandon ship. The Michelin dreams I once had quickly became my *Nightmare on Elm Street*. While I remained committed to doing the best job I could while charting my new course, regret lingered in my mind. Had I made the right decision? I had doubts. What happened next can only be explained as divine intervention.

The owner wanted to host a wine dinner, which had been met with previous success. It was guaranteed money when profits were down. I didn't feel it was cutting edge enough to help us turn the corner as a business; we needed a shock to the system. This wasn't the time to play it safe. I wanted to do something outside the box.

"What if we showcased foods from around the world instead of wines?" I suggested. "We could create a global street food tour in one evening."

Then the owner said something I'll never forget: "We're spending my money, and we'll do whatever I think. When it's your money, you can do whatever you'd like."

I had been dismissed even though my intentions were good. I wanted to help his restaurant survive. I wanted his restaurant to be one of the greatest in the country. It was my dream job, and I was ready for the fight. I had been willing to train the staff. I had been willing to deal with broken equipment. I was giving everything I had.

His retort (dismissive as it was) was persuasive, and he was right. It was time to go out on my own.

Brother Luck's guest appearance showcasing his creole heritage at Comal Food Incubator in Denver, CO. (2018) Dana Keith

Ten years later, as I reflect on that experience, I see things differently. Succeeding in business has little to do with your passion or willingness to work. Talent and determination mean nothing if you cannot manage people, products, and, most importantly, profits—if it doesn't make dollars, then it doesn't make sense.

But all three need each other in order to work. Do you have the right people around you? Are you continuing your education to stay relevant in the marketplace and deliver on your promise to your customers? Are you being advised on how to manage the money? Don't trust your own cleverness. Seek counsel. Listen to those who have gone before you. And whatever you do, care about the people even if it is at the expense of your product and your profits.

17. POP-UP DINNERS

All hard work brings a profit, but mere talk leads only to poverty.

A chef's mind works in crisis mode and solves problems every day. We're constantly anticipating what could go wrong and taking the needed steps to prevent it from happening.

How many pieces of asparagus do I have?
Did I double-check the count on shrimp?
What's plan B if I get an unexpected vegan guest tonight?
Can I serve plates and cook the third course if my staff doesn't show?
Whom can I call to help at the last minute?
Who dropped this oven temperature to 250 degrees?
What can I substitute for that course if the pork doesn't get tender enough?

And that's just during the prep or before the first guest arrives. Have you ever wondered what it's like inside a chef's mind during a busy service?

Fire two more orders of chicken; we're short! Now!

Did you seriously just drop the pan of Brussels? Fire another one and check that chicken.

Good job on the reduction; it's money! This emulsification is perfect.

I need more hands in the window to serve! It's so freaking hot in here.

Where's my side towel? Did you take my spoon?

I think that chicken needs to cook for a few more minutes.

Somebody hand me more plates! Why is this taking so long?

Can someone grab me a quart container of ice water?

Where's the garnish tray?

Why is there water in the sliced chives?

I hate these stupid tweezers. What am I? A surgeon?

This is taking too long. Everybody hates everything.

Look at their body language. That lady is definitely not impressed.

Why did the last couple of plates come back half empty? Did they not like the grits?

I need to check the salt on that sauce.

This ticket machine is going to haunt my dreams.

Be careful and do not break any more plates. Those things are so expensive!

Why is there never a food runner when I need one?

This table needs to be walked immediately so I can begin working on the next few tickets.

I need a bigger expo window. Heat lamps are so freaking expensive!

Someone grab me more fleur de salt! Ready to walk table 32.

Only 342 more plates to serve; I shouldn't have looked at the clock.

Damn, it's only 6:45 pm: I wish I smoked so I could get a break.

As the to-do lists and unpaid bills piled up, my mind raced

more and more. Frustrated by the lack of support at the magical property tucked into the hillside of Manitou Springs but inspired by our owner's clarity of mind, it was time to start my own business.

I was thirty; Tina had just thrown me a surprise party, and my life seemed to be flittering away. I was teetering on the edge of a cliff.

My stomach fluttered with butterflies as I imagined the free-fall. In the days following, my brain asked one question over and over again: Will you jump off the cliff or what?

I wanted to do something different. I needed something that was ultimately a reflection of me. I decided to host a pop-up dinner. My good friend Eric suggested a location:

"You'll love this space," he said. "My family has owned this bar for ten years. My uncle doesn't really use the kitchen too much."

Eric was talking about the Triple Nickel Tavern, a downtown bar I had visited only a couple of times. It was small but perfect. The irony was I had tried to lease this same place the year before.

"You could host your first pop-up dinner in the Triple Nickel," Eric said as he looked at me excitedly.

I could tell he was feeling the idea of me hosting an exclusive dinner. Eric had previously worked for me at Cheyenne Mountain Resort, and we became close friends.

"You should do your street foods from all over the world idea there," he continued.

"I'll call it Street Eats," I replied with the enthusiasm of a child writing his list to Santa.

We continued brainstorming: What did I want the guests to experience? How was I going to advertise it and take reservations? What would the menu be?

My first restaurant was unexpectedly born in Eric's living room. My life was about to change. I knew I was risking it all. I decided to go big and compose an eight-course menu:

Street Eats Pop-Up Menu

First
Chicharron Tacos & Elotes

Second
Hot and Sour Beef Short Rib Soup

Third
Octopus Satay

Fourth
Bone Marrow Tator Tots

Fifth
Chicken and Waffles with Whipped Hot Sauce

Sixth
Buffalo Corn Dog with Blood Orange Ketchup

Seventh
Green Chile Bruschetta

Eighth
Curry Scented Cotton Candy

After leaving Eric's house, I spent the rest of the night typing. I created a marketing flyer and posted it to my blog:[1]

crEATe719 kitchen presents a "Pop Up Restaurant" – June 23rd, 2013 @ Triple Nickel Tavern. Hosted by Chef Brother Luck. $45 per person. Includes local beer cocktail pairings. Tickets available on the following Eventbrite link.

I discovered way back then that I enjoy writing: it is story-telling, it is inspirational, but most importantly, it is self-discovery.

Brother Luck collaborating in a ChefsFeed Indie Week dinner featuring 24 chefs from across the country in downtown Nashville. Pictured Above, Chef Megan Sanchez of Guero Portland, OR, and Chef Johnny Rhodes of Restaurant Indigo Houston, TX. (2019) ChefsFeed

The following day I woke up full of nervous energy. I had decided on the date, and with the announcement made, I moved into marketing. I tagged every media persona in that first post; I figured they had the platforms to share it with the masses. Next, I set up a Facebook Event page and invited every person I knew in Colorado Springs.

We sold out in twenty-four hours; I was onto something. Colorado Springs lacked foodie events, and there was a demand. People had told me the city was not ready for this style of food: organ meats, molecular, farm to table, poetry on the plate. I was about to prove them wrong. It was all me and my imagination. I was finally in charge of everything. I was testing the idea of becoming a restaurateur.

My next dilemma was equipment; where would I get plates, silverware, glasses, and napkins on the cheap? The questions just kept rolling in: How would I serve the drinks? Whom can I get to work in the kitchen? Who would serve the tables? Where was I going to get tables and chairs? And there was shopping to be done. Could I pull this off? I still needed to test the menu!

"We killed it!" I exclaimed to everyone who helped me host my first pop-up dinner; the satisfied smiles of our guests confirmed the delighted palettes. People who believed in me stood with me. I wasn't the only one jumping off a cliff that day: Tina enlisted our niece, Amy, and Eric's wife, Amanda, to serve. Eric and my brother, Slade, helped me in the kitchen.

Tina Luck serving powdered peanut butter and jelly shots at the Willy Wonka pop-up dinner. (2013)

I was exhausted. My clogs were worn from the repetitive steps throughout the tiny kitchen. An internal decision had been made. After cleaning up the kitchen, I found the owner sitting at the bar.

We sealed the deal with a handshake followed by a shot of tequila. My first restaurant cost me $500 a month. Brother Luck Street Eats had a home. I clutched the door key as I walked to my truck. Monday morning was officially going to be my first day as a restauranteur.

I recall being extremely nervous. Not being able to sleep. It felt like it was my first day of high school. At 5:00 a.m., I creased sharp lines into my chef coat. I wanted to look the part. I glanced at the checklist I had jotted in my notebook; doing so would become part of my daily routine for much of the next year.

- Carniceria: grab octopus, nopales, onions, chiles, and masa
- Asian Pacific Market: pick up gochujang, rice noodles, miso paste, chicken feet, and duck eggs.
- Costco: dairy, dry goods, eggs, and produce.
- Walmart: Paper goods, misc. ingredients, office supplies
- Dollar Tree: More plates, glassware, and bowls
- United Restaurant Supply: Kitchen equipment
- Home Depot: Screws, light bulbs, cleaning supplies

During those long ten months, I wrote the daily menu based on what I had sourced. If I ended up touring someone's garden, I'd ask to cut herbs and flowers. Whenever a vendor stopped by with samples, they would end up on that evening's menu. I couldn't afford to waste anything. I butchered whole chickens and ducks to craft entrees, used the innards to make pate, roasted the bones to make soup, and toasted the skin to make cracklins. I was balling on a budget every day in that little kitchen.

Every night there was a concert of sorts, literally. There was a stage just outside my mini kingdom, and it proudly hosted punk rock bands from all over the country. This little bar had more of a reputation than I did.

Once the smoke cleared and the mosh pits, mohawks, and

leather jackets departed, I addressed the aftermath. Every night, with my kitchen cleaned, I'd put tomorrow morning's hand-written shopping list in my back pocket and start the cleanup. I'd start by waking up the guy sleeping in the corner, then repair the tables broken during a fight. I'd patch the fist-sized holes in the wall. (I quickly learned the futility of scrubbing graffiti off the walls or peeling away promotional stickers.) The bathrooms were the worst; let's just say it's even more horrifying during the daytime. Finding bloody heroin needles at 9:00 a.m. is way too much reality that early in the day.

At some point, Tina and I started discussing the idea of relo-cating into a better space. We needed something larger. The expe-rience we were trying to deliver in the back of this punk rock bar was never going to happen. This wasn't the ideal space for my restaurant, and I knew it.

When that voice inside your head tells you to listen, do you? I feel like I'm less in control when I'm trying to control everything. Do you feel the same way? Jumping off the ledge is seriously the hardest part. Falling is easy. You've got to learn to trust yourself when making decisions. How? By making decisions, reflecting on the outcomes, and asking others for feedback. Seriously, if you are going to jump, make sure you have great people around you who know how to fly.

18. STREET EATS WAS NO DIVE

Do not boast about tomorrow,
for you do not know what a day may bring.

The text message came from one of my wine reps, Staci
Blair, who knew I was trying to find a way to grow beyond
the small kitchen of the Triple Nickel Tavern. I was intrigued by
the attached photos.

Staci: Hey Chef. I think I found the
perfect space for you to move into. It's a
small restaurant on the west side. I'll
send some pictures for you to check out.

Brother Luck: Where is it on the west
side?

Staci: A small place called Ramon Q's
Cantina. It's on 10th Street and Colorado

```
Ave. Do you want me to introduce you to
the owners?
```

```
Brother Luck: Sure… that'd be great.
```

The following week, Tina and I met the owners to tour this small yellow house that had been converted into a restaurant. It was cozy.

The iron fencing encased the front yard with a Eurocentric trellised entry overrun with grapevines. Thirty patio chairs and tables sat on stone slabs adjacent to a beautiful fountain encircled with gravel.

"What an awkward layout for a restaurant," Tina whispered as we walked to our table.

I quickly agreed. The floor plan wasn't ideal. It only sat thirty people and had an awkward granite stone bar just inside the entrance. There was only one restroom. But it was better than what we were working with at the bar.

After lunch, the owners sat down with us to discuss their situation and reason for vacating.

"We've taken on the responsibilities of raising our siblings' children and cannot operate a restaurant as well," said the wife.

"The space has been good to us over the last few years, but we need to put all of our time into these kids," added the husband. "We could put together an equipment inventory and transfer the lease."

They were a nice couple that seemed to have good intentions. After a few weeks of negotiating and praying, Tina and I decided to jump. We signed a three-year lease in May 2014 and paid the couple $20,000 for all their equipment.

Brother hanging his restaurant sign at the new location of Brother Luck Street Eats. (2013) Tina Luck

"Where's my food for the six top on the patio?" yelled Tina as I frantically plated bacon jam burgers and slung them into the window.

"We're going down out here, and Amy is drowning," Tina continued.

Our poor niece was serving tables for us and was completely overwhelmed. We were getting rocked. The entire patio was packed, and so was every seat in the restaurant. The wait to be seated was well over an hour, and our point-of-sale system had crashed.

We opened Street Eats only three weeks after signing the lease and closing operations at the bar. Tina and I enlisted friends to paint the walls in exchange for beer and lunch. I had written an elaborate menu that was overly complicated for the newly-hired staff. We had our liquor license, and our bar was stocked with a plethora of alcohol. There was no real training; we didn't even have recipes for the food or drinks. I had leaped off another giant cliff with the expectation that everyone was just as crazy as myself. There was no bottom to this cliff. It was only clouds and dreams. I launched off the ledge without programming the point-of-sale system, and now we were all paying for my adrenaline-junkie desires.

"Where's that gnocchi and cheese?" I yelled to the sauté station.

"Coming, Chef," replied the poor cook who had been sweating nonstop for the last five hours.

We were bushwhacking through some tall brush, and my machete felt dull as a spoon. Tina decided to stop bussing tables, so we couldn't seat anyone else. She was now at the front door telling the excited crowd awaiting dinner from the new Chef

Brother Luck restaurant that we wouldn't be able to serve them tonight. I had failed. This was one of the worst services I had ever worked. I was eating some serious humble pie. At that point in my career, I knew I was a talented chef but had no concept of what it took to run a restaurant.

Brother creating a "table-side" bone marrow at his restaurant Street Eats *inspired by an Alinea dessert experience. (2016) Will Rutledge*

We were about a year into the new Street Eats location, and I had finally started finding my rhythm. I was feeling confident in the food we were executing. Dinner services were pretty busy, and lunch was decent. Brunch had a strong following, but I was burning the candle on both ends.

I scheduled myself to open the kitchen each morning until another team member arrived at noon. I set up the kitchen for the day and prepped all of the *mise en place* (meaning everything in its place) for the lunch service. Once the first cook showed up, I floated between preparing food in the kitchen and running plates to the guests. If things got hectic, I also bussed tables. I can remember the shock on people's faces as I took their orders and cleaned the dirty dishes off the table next to them.

When you're the owner, you do it all: you don't have a choice. It's your money and reputation on the line. Every plate. Every guest. Every second feels like you're standing on a bridge made of glass; at any moment, the sound of cracking could commence, resulting in a downward spiral toward a kamikaze-like death.

Not Meeting Guy Fieri

One day during lunch service, a team member poked his head into the kitchen and said, "Hey chef, someone is on the phone asking to speak with the owner. They said something about Guy Fieri's *Diners, Dives, and Drives.*"

I looked at the other cook in the kitchen and shrugged. At the time, I wasn't a fan of the show. Guy Fieri was the hottest thing on Food Network, and I felt pretty dismissive about his content. I felt like most of the restaurants featured were gimmicks or niche restaurants.

I was a chef. I wanted to be the next Thomas Keller. I wore a chef coat and carried a severe ego.

"Good afternoon, and thank you for calling *Brother Luck Street Eats*. This is Brother Luck. How may I be of service?" I answered the phone.

"Hi, Brother. I'm a casting producer for Guy Fieri's television show *Diners, Drive-Ins and Dives*. We're coming to Colorado Springs and would love to feature your restaurant. We received some positive reviews about your food."

"I'm not interested in being on the show, but thank you for calling and considering us," I calmly and confidently replied. I quickly hung up the phone and looked at my team, who were huddled around me.

"Did you seriously just decline Guy Fieri?" asked the cook.

"I sure did. We're better than that, and I don't think we fit the profile of who they feature."

My ego was at an all-time high, and the expectations I measured myself against were not Guy Fieri. I would soon regret this decision.

Guy Fieri came to town a few months later, and Colorado Springs went crazy. Every newscast was about the restaurants he would be featuring. Lines were out the door for these businesses as they all hoped to catch a glimpse of the spiky-haired chef filming his iconic show.

My Twitter feed had been blowing up nonstop with comments from the community.

Why aren't you @chefbrotherluck #streeteats @guyfieri?

The best place to get food is with @chefbrotherluck.

@guyfieri needs to go see @chefbrotherluck #coloradosprings.

I didn't know how to respond to all these passionate comments promoting our business. I couldn't just say I was an egomaniac who had declined to do the show. I felt like an idiot because my restaurant was almost empty while he was in town.

I didn't realize the power of the celebrity chef until Guy Fieri came to Colorado Springs. There was a lack of representation for our food community, which led to everyone's excitement— supply and demand. Locals (especially the restaurant employees) were going crazy trying to meet a celebrity chef.

I realized that because the community wanted more out of our local food scene, I might be able to become the celebrity chef who could not only promote our city but represent them. As I said, I had a pretty healthy (unhealthy) ego.

Still frustrated by my foolish rejection of Guy Fieri, I was in Manhatten with Oliver Malcolm, a former C-CAP student I had mentored while I was in Chicago. Oliver had won a scholarship which included a trip to New York to spend a week exploring the restaurant culture of the city, and he invited me to join him. One of our stops was a visit with Damien Mogavero, a successful hospitality businessman. I shared with him my story about declining to be featured on *Diners, Drive-Ins and Dives*; his response changed my mentality about television and cooking:

"In business, you need to remove your ego. It's not about what you like or prefer. You're serving a guest who has their preferences. They all want to share the story of dining in a celebrity restaurant. You just declined national exposure from a global brand. You could have lived off that feature for the next three years, and it wouldn't have cost you anything. This is business, and you need to get your feelings out the way if you want it to be successful."

I'll never forget sitting in a downtown Manhattan boardroom listening to his disapproval.

During the four-hour flight back to Colorado, my ego and I made a pact: I would become a the chef ambassador Colorado Springs needed. People would be excited to meet me like they were for Guy Fieri. They would ask me for selfies and to sign their menus. I was going to make my city proud: My business mindset needed to change!

The sixteen-year-old inside me had just found the next cliff to jump off.

Over the years, my hard-headedness has always gotten in my

way. I'm sure many of you know this feeling. Are you one of those that knows it all? At times, I definitely am. I have to keep great people around me who can help manage my ego. It's way too easy to get lost in pride and arrogance. Trust me; I've been there over and over.

19. CHOPPED

Fools give full vent to their rage,
but the wise bring calm in the end.

I had flown to San Francisco to spend time with Tina before my travel schedule ramped up. She was attending a work conference, and we were excited to spend some time touring the city in which I was raised.

I grimaced as we entered our hotel room, and looking at Tina, I mumbled, "My tooth is killing me!"

"You should go get it checked out when we get home," she responded.

"I don't think I can wait that long. I still need to do the Bacon Festival, then fly straight to New York for the *Chopped* episode." Something was wrong with my tooth, and I wasn't going to make it with another week left on the road.

As she got ready for her work meetings, I got ready for my day. I intended to wander around the city and relive the sounds and sights I remembered from my childhood. "I think I'm going for a walk while you're in meetings today," was all I could muster to Tina.

It had been twenty-seven years since I had walked the streets of the city. Stepping out onto the sidewalk, I texted my cousin: "What was the address of the apartment my parents had?" (He had recently sent me a picture on his last trip to the Bay Area.)

I had mixed emotions as I approached the apartment building where I had spent much of my childhood. It now had been converted into a beautiful condo. I sat on the street curb across from the front door. I was startled by a sudden memory of the San Francisco Earthquake of 1989. I could almost feel the sidewalk churn underneath me as I remembered feeling the floor shaking and hearing kitchen pots and pans fall to the floor.

Slade and I were entertaining ourselves with our toys as my father watched the World Series: the Oakland Athletics were playing the San Francisco Giants in the Battle of the Bay. One moment my mother was cooking, and the next, she was hurling us under the kitchen table. When it all stopped, we ran outside. The whole neighborhood gathered around a mobile black-and-white portable television plugged into a car's cigarette lighter and watched as the local news reported the devastation. The bay bridge's upper tier had collapsed onto the lower level. People were falling into the water below. Streets had been split wide open, and large pieces of buildings were falling onto unsuspecting patrons below.

I don't know where a bad memory ends and PTSD begins, but I am sure this qualifies as trauma for a child. The sounds of people crying, screaming, and discussing the recent earthquake will live in my brain forever.

With the trip down memory lane over, it was time to focus. Not only had I come back to San Francisco for a date with my wife and a moment of reflection, but I was closing the gap on a missed opportunity: tomorrow, I would be cooking on stage with Guy Fieri in front of a live audience. The Bacon Festival would be my moment to correct the mistake I had at Street Eats.

Bacon

The mobile stage reminded me of Optimus Prime from my favorite childhood cartoon, *The Transformers*. The seventy-foot platform was towed in by a large black semi-truck. After the push of a button, two professional-grade custom competition kitchens appeared, followed by an eighteen-foot jumbotron centered above the roll-out stage.

I was invited to compete in a professional chef mystery basket challenge at the Bacon Festival hosted at the Dell Osso Family Farm in Lathrop, California, just outside the Bay Area. Guy Fieri was the host, and I would make sure I made a good impression this time.

Arriving at the competition, I carried my knife roll and a heap of regret. Just a year before, I had turned down an opportunity to be featured on *Diners, Drive-Ins and Dives*. Over the last year, I had been cooking on Food Network pretty consistently. I beat Bobby Flay. Robert Irvine filmed a special episode of *Chopped* with me and a few others in New York, and my restaurant was featured on a new show called *Cooks vs. Cons*. Today was my chance to add Guy Fieri to the list.

There was an expected audience of over 5,000 people, and I was going to be cooking live on stage with one of the most famous chefs on the planet. Would Guy be approachable? I hoped he wasn't going to be one of those "Don't talk to me, I'm famous" celebrities. I showed my badge and stepped behind the stage; entering the green room, I immediately recognized that iconic spiky blond hair.

"How you doing brotha?" Guy asked candidly.

Did he know my name, or was he just offering "How you doing brotha?" as a friendly greeting. I've been greeted this way for years and still don't know how to respond to the ambiguity.

I responded to Guy the only way I could, "I'm good. It's a pleasure to meet you."

Guy started talking about basketball and how he was taking his sons to the Golden State Warriors game that evening. I'm a huge fan of the team; having this commonality with Guy put me at ease. I snapped a selfie with Guy before picking up my knives and heading to my station on the transformer stage. It was time to compete; I swallowed the nerves and stepped into the spotlight. It wasn't *Diners, Drive-Ins and Dives*, but I was grateful to have the opportunity to be on the same stage as Guy Fieri, albeit in California and not in my restaurant in Colorado Springs.

Guy Fieri and Brother Luck taking a photo at the Dell'Osso farm in Lathrop, CA, before the Bacon and Beer Festival. (2016)

Chopped and Blue Tape

I rolled over and reached for my phone. What time was it? I had stayed up late watching Game Seven of the NBA Finals—the Warriors had lost. I resonated with the feeling because I had lost the competition at the Bacon Festival.

Guy Fieri was hilarious to watch as he hosted the mystery basket challenge. When it came time to announce the winner, my name wasn't called. I walked off the stage and, having exorcised a demon, I proudly shook Guy's hand.

But now, at 4:47 a.m., I was running late for my flight to Denver. I jumped up, grabbed my bags, and sprinted out the door.

My head and tooth were throbbing as I arrived at the counter to check my suitcase (and my favorite knives).

"Your bag will not make the plane at this point," the attendant informed me.

I had missed the cutoff time to check my luggage.

I planned to fly to New York with a layover in Denver. I was heading to Manhattan to film an episode of *Chopped*. I needed my knives for the show and would not make my connecting flight if I had to wait for them to arrive on the next flight from San Francisco to Denver. "Fine, just put them on the next flight, and I'll figure it out when I land in Denver," I told the attendant. She handed me my boarding pass, and I ran toward security and then to the gate.

"Thank you for being patient," were the only words I could sheepishly muster as I shuffled onto the plane. Everyone was staring at me, but I didn't care. Somehow I had made the flight.

I was hungover, out of breath, and none of my luggage had made the plane, but I did. As we took off, I looked at the San Francisco Bay below. I was on my way to New York for the next leg of my journey: I had no knives, clothes, or toiletries. And the trip was just getting started.

During my layover in Denver, I arranged to have my luggage and my knives delivered to my house in Colorado Springs as they wouldn't make it to New York on time. Then I called the C-CAP office in Manhattan, told them my situation, and asked, "Do you have a starter set that you usually give high school kids?"

"We've got you, Chef. Let me see what I can do, and don't worry; by the time you land, there will be knives at your hotel. Where are you staying?" replied the C-CAP coordinator.

Everything was working itself out. I needed to get some pain medication for my tooth. Tylenol and Ibuprofen weren't cutting it. I called my brother-in-law, who is also my pharmacist. "Can you schedule a pickup for my pain medication at a location near my hotel in New York?" I asked. With the knives arranged and the prescription called in, I made a list of what I would need for the next two days: black pants, nonslip black shoes, socks, underwear, t-shirts, toothpaste, toothbrush, and deodorant.

The city of lights turned dark when I saw the closed sign at the pharmacy inside Walgreens. My tooth must have felt the panic because it doubled down on the pain. Filming would not be fun if I couldn't soothe the pain. I grabbed a tube of over the counter pain relief gel and placed it on the register with my toiletries. Next up, clothing.

My phone beeped as I walked out of the store. I looked down at the voicemail notification and hit listen. "Hey Chef, I spoke with the team at Korin, and they've sent a custom set of knives to your hotel. Please let me know when you get them, and good luck on *Chopped* in the morning."

At least that part was solved. I smiled because I'd be traveling to Japan with the Korin team in a few weeks; I was grateful for their gesture. As a fine importer of Japanese knives and purveyor of various culinary goods, I knew the knives from Korin would serve me well during tomorrow's competition.

Times Square was animated as always. Street hustlers were selling CDs, knock-off purses, and fake jewelry. The tourists scrambled about looking like the perfect victims. You can always tell a tourist in a major city because their heads are always looking up. City folk already know the skyscrapers are tall.

I wandered into a men's clothing store and shuttered with disgust as I picked up a pair of black jeans—$279 for a pair of jeans I needed to cook in? No way: it was time to find a Ross where I could purchase everything I needed for under $100. After grabbing the remaining items on my list, I headed toward my hotel.

I picked up the immaculate Japanese knife set left by the Korin team at the front desk and headed to my room. My jaw hurt, and I needed some sleep. I put the gel on my gums and popped a few more ibuprofen. I turned the television on and found Food Network. I drifted into sleep as I listened to Ted Allen tell the contestants about the ingredients in their mystery boxes. Tomorrow I would be one of those contestants. Bacon, hard-boiled eggs, Nutella, and gefilte fish? What could I make with those components?

I arrived at a coffee shop in the Chelsea Market area of Manhattan to meet the Food Network team at 6:00 a.m. Walking in, I was greeted by a smile from the barista and the whooshing sound of steaming milk. As I ordered a latte, I scanned the crowd, searching for any indication of who could be a cook. Who was going to be my competition? Who had no hair on their arms? Who looked like they never get up this early and most likely went to bed only a few hours ago?

The first contestant was easy to recognize; she wore kitchen clogs and carried a knife roll. I walked over and introduced myself. Within a few minutes, the other two competitors walked in. A young producer greeted us with too much enthusiasm for zero-dark-early: "Are you all excited to compete on *Chopped?*" she asked.

We all nodded in agreement as the butterflies in my stomach began to flutter.

We departed the coffee shop to begin what would be a long day of filming. The morning buzz of the city started to come to life as commuters rushed to punch the clock. And for the four of us, the show was about to begin.

"Please put on these black shirts and butcher aprons. We will begin filming shortly. All of your cell phones and personal belongings need to be stored in these lockers while you're filming today," said the producer, a little less bubbly than before.

I felt nervous, but I always feel anxious when I'm about to

compete. My jaw was still hurting, and the over-the-counter medicine was barely helping. I would have to embrace my pain for now and cry about it later. Today was my chance at redemption after losing the Bacon Festival competition in California only a couple of days before.

As I arrived in the competition kitchen of this iconic show, I took notes of the station and pantry area. There was water boiling on my stovetop, and the oven had been preheated to full blast. The dry pantry was stocked with spices, produce, grains, and molecular ingredients. Every kitchen tool was arranged perfectly on the wire shelving: whisks, spoons, spatulas, tongs, and pastry bags. There was the dreaded ice cream machine, which I knew to stay away from, and an anti-griddle that makes it possible to freeze ingredients on a negative thirty-degree surface: this was going to be fun! The pain in my jaw and the nerves were beginning to subside as my excitement about competing grew.

"Please stand on these marks and do not open your baskets until the director asks," the producer asked as she pointed to the blue tape lining the floors.

After a moment of anxious waiting, our host Ted Allen strolled in with today's judges, Scott Conant, Alex Guarnaschelli, and Maneet Chauhan. I was familiar with all three and was excited to cook for them. Scott is an Italian chef renowned for his disgust for raw onions and innovative styles. Alex is known as a fierce competitor and earned the title of Iron Chef. Maneet intrigued me the most: I had recently eaten at her restaurant in Nashville—Chauhan Ale & Masala House—and was enamored by her mingling of Indian and Southern cuisines. I don't think I could have asked for a better caliber of judges who would be evaluating my cooking and creativity as we filmed this episode of *Chopped*.

"If your dish doesn't cut it, you will be chopped. Are you ready to see what basket beasts await you?" announced Ted Allen as we prepared to begin the first round. "You've got sekacz, kale, chicken liver, and chickens on a spit. Twenty minutes to work, and the time starts now!"

My mind began to race. What the heck is sekacz? As the clock started to tick, I immediately tasted the sekacz. To paraphrase Alex Guarnaschelli, "It's like cornbread crashed into a lemon pound cake." I decided to incorporate it into a churro and serve it with a chicken liver mousse.

I removed the chicken breast from the carcass and lightly poached a few slices to warm it through but not cook it any further. The roasted chicken was awful because it was ice cold and super bland. I guess that was the point of the challenge.

Turning my attention to the final ingredient, I decided to make fried kale chips. My dish was coming together fairly quickly, and I wanted to make sure I used every mystery ingredient. I started to plate my dish with the sekacz churro.

I had toasted the cake and tossed it into an orange chili sugar mixture. The chicken liver mousse was sexy and smooth. I filled the center and placed the poached chicken breast on top with a pinch of sea salt. The kale chips would add perfect texture as my final garnish.

"Time's up, chefs," announced Ted Allen as we all placed our hands in the air. I was sweating heavily but felt confident in the dish I had just plated.

As we landed on our blue tape to receive critiques from the judges, I received positive reviews. Maneet said the sugar I added "made it inherently sweet, but it was overall a good dish." Scott and Alex both agreed it was a well-conceived dish.

After listening to the judges' comments on the remaining dishes, we were presented with the silver-domed plate to reveal who would be chopped. I closed my eyes as the lid was removed. I was relieved when I dared to look at the judges' table. I had not been chopped during the first round.

Ted laughed as he announced the ingredients for round two: "Let's see what's in the baskets? You've got white chocolate curry cashews, butternut squash, goat's milk yogurt, and whole roasted goats." We were all shaken by whole roasted animals propped up on the butcher table in front of us.

I started with the goat: it was easily the toughest ingredient in more ways than one, as it can be tough and stringy if not braised for a long time. I butchered off the backstrap as it is likely to be the most tender cut on the animal.

I began to char the meat on cast iron to build texture and was determined not to cook it any longer than necessary. I then turned my attention to preparing a butternut squash puree to provide a gorgeous color on the plate and a silky-smooth texture.

I softened the white chocolate curry cashews by boiling them and glazed them with a sugar crunch, and I used the liquid to sweeten the apple chutney. (Making chutney for one of the most famous Indian chefs was risky, but I felt confident.)

I started plating my dish after blending my butternut squash puree with the goat's milk yogurt; I placed the squash dead center and topped it with a slice of charred goat meat. Next, I added the apple chutney that rounded out the dish by adding a whimsical flavor profile of sweet, spicy, salty, and sour.

I finished the plate with a few candied cashews and some charred bitter lettuce. This dish was money, and I knew it as Ted called "Times up. Please step back."

When the judging began, Maneet was the first to speak up: "Love the presentation. It's a very sophisticated presentation which makes it very inviting. The butternut squash puree with the chutney is spot on."

With her affirming words about my rendition of a dish from her own country, I could breathe again.

Alex Guarnaschelli jumped in next to offer her opinions: "The apple combination is something you should put on your menu, and when you do, I will come eat it with eighty of my friends. It is so good."

Brother picking fresh herbs from his garden outside his restaurant Four by Brother Luck. (2018) Dana Keith

Wow! "So far, so good," was all I was thinking. I knew this dish was solid, and I was glad they were enjoying it as well as I had hoped.

Scott chimed in with his thoughts: "Beautiful presentation for the second dish in a row. Really, really nice. You clearly have a cerebral way of looking at food. I think the technique of charring the goat was not the best choice for heating it. You seared it so hard it became super stringy and tough. There's a lot of stuff happening with flavor but not the goat."

When it came time to lift the silver lid again to discover who would be chopped, I knew it wouldn't be me. As the lid was removed, I learned the judges agreed. I was going to the third and final dessert round.

At this point, we had been filming for about six hours, and my tooth was starting to bother me again. I had made it to the final round and was about to begin one last battle. The chef I was competing against was also from Colorado and highly talented.

Backstage, after the first round, we joked that we knew it would come down to us. He was friendly but still presented an air that screamed, "I want to win just as badly as you do, so prepare for war!"

We lined up on those pieces of blue tape and waited for the next basket.

The episode was titled *Beast Feast,* so I was sure there would be another animal for the dessert round. I prayed it wasn't another roasted bland animal.

"Chef Chris and Chef Brother, our meat fest is not quite done yet. Open your final baskets. You'll be making desserts with marrow chutney, fresh figs, bacon, and too big to fit in the baskets; whole pigs," announced Ted Allen.

Are you freaking serious? What was I going to do with this demon spawn of a pig that had been roasted in the flames of hell? As I glanced at the pig, it looked so shriveled and sad. I felt good about the other ingredients. The figs were a cakewalk. I would simply macerate them in some sugar and vinegar with a touch of extra virgin olive oil. (I've never been a fan of overly sweet desserts.)

You can't have a *Beast Feast* without bacon, so that was no surprise. I would make my signature bacon jam utilizing three of the ingredients. The bacon and roasted pork would be caramelized with molasses, balsamic, wine, and brown sugar. Marrow chutney would help bind all of the pork together since it was a squash-based accouterment from Australia.

I decided to fill wontons with my bacon jam and deep fry them. The figs would add freshness to the crispy pastry. And I'd brulee them to add deep caramel flavor. Wanting to add a creamy texture to contrast the crunch of the wonton, I blended ricotta with agave nectar. And to prevent it from being too sweet, I chopped fresh rosemary to add a savory component.

As I plated the dessert, I glanced up to view the clock: My dish was coming together nicely. What seemed like just seconds later, I heard, "Time's up. Please step back." All that kept going through my head was, Will this dish win? Is it a $10,000 dessert?

I described my dish to the judges and prepared for the onslaught of professional opinions.

"Love the figs; I love the fact that you bruleed it. It gives it a little bit more of the smokiness," observed Maneet.

"The flavors really work well together. I love the sweetness of the bacon jam inside the wonton. I'm not crazy about the rosemary inside of the ricotta," stated Scott.

Well, two down and the toughest one to go. Alex Guarnaschelli has a remarkable way of carrying the most intense poker face. It's like she's staring straight into your soul and having a conversation with St. Peter about every sin you've ever committed before creating this dish. It's funny because, after this experience, I've often studied her mannerisms to improve my performance while on camera. She's truly an inspiration.

Alex announced, "I like this dessert a lot, but I agree with Scott on the rosemary. I don't like the texture of the ricotta in here. That said, the flavors are great."

It was official. I had competed in all three rounds of an episode of Food Network's *Chopped*. I now needed to wait while the judges deliberated on our entire performance.

Chef Chris and I were guided to a different set to discuss the round and reflect on our performances. After a few interviews and comedic dialogue for the cameras, we were brought back to the judges' table.

Ted Allen made his dramatic intro to the judges' decision "So, whose dish is on the chopping block? Chef Brother, you've been chopped."

I felt like a total failure. I had lost the Bacon Festival with Guy Fieri, and I had lost my episode of *Chopped*. I had embarked on this journey a week ago with hopes of grandeur and applause. My wife was supportive of the crazy itinerary. What did I have to show for it?

I was devastated to hear I had been chopped. My blood began to boil like the squash I had just been simmering, and I exploded upon my exit. The producer had asked me to do my walk of shame down the fake hallway for my outro, and I couldn't control my emotions. I pushed the swinging door with more strength than I meant to and knocked the wall back, shaking the entire set. The producer asked me to calm down.

My exit interviews were short and straight to the point. I was at my wit's end and didn't have anything left. I didn't understand how I had just lost. How did I just blow $10,000? Italy was off the table for Tina, all because I had failed.

Maya Angelou, the American poet, actress, and an important figure in the American Civil Rights Movement, once said, "You may encounter many defeats, but you must not be defeated. In fact, it may be necessary to encounter the defeats, so you can know who you are, what you can rise from, how you can still come out of it." These back-to-back losses are just two of my many encounters with defeat. So often, I have deemed myself to be a failure. But is it true? Am I a failure because I lost? Are you a failure because you can't get over your past or fear the future? No! We are people who have taken risks, and we have failed.

There is another lie in the world that says you are the sum of your past sins and you will be remembered for your worst moments. I've had my share of them, and so have you. But we are not failures. We are men and women who have failed. I have learned to reflect on these defeats and learn from them. More often than not, I needed someone to give me a little perspective so I didn't remain consumed in the lie. This night was no different.

I'm glad I had a thirty-block walk back to my hotel because I needed it to cool off. I called Tina to tell her I had lost, and her voice and support were a comfort to me. I went to bed agitated but hopeful. Tomorrow would be another blank page where I could begin writing a new chapter. I started it by returning the knives to Korin.

20. A MOTHER'S COIN

Let the wise hear and increase in learning,
and the one who understands obtain guidance...

I became enamored with Japan while growing up in San Francisco; many nights, I would dream of cherry blossoms and Hirohito coins. My parents had spent time traveling through Tokyo before I was born, and their stories and numerous photo albums grew my world beyond our apartment.

We regularly visited Japantown, where I peered into the water and made suckling fish sounds while staring at the brightly colored coins strewn about the bottom of the Koi pond. The aroma of cherry trees delighted my nose; the soft pink of the flowering tree calmed me as I walked through the gardens. And images of the five-tiered peace pagoda remind me of home as much as any memory of the Golden Gate Bridge.

It was with my mom that I first had sushi; I remember giggling as she ordered the purple octopus tentacles. And we would always stop at a small market to buy strawberry-covered Pocky. I'm sure my love of exotic foods comes from her adventurous spirit and desire to help me travel the world without leaving the Bay Area.

As we strolled the sidewalks, she enthusiastically recounted her trips to Japan and gave me glimpses into their life there. "Your dad loved the sumo wrestlers. He would stalk them like a fangirl."

There was something special about Japan. My mom spoke pretty good Japanese. She taught me to count from one to ten: *ichi, ni, san, shi, go, roku, shichi, hachi, kyuu, juu.* And we would rehearse greetings to each other: *ko-nee-chee-wah, a-rri-gato, si-or-nara.* And she gave me a 100 yen coin and told me to spend it whenever I made it to Tokyo.

Though I knew my parents loved Japan, I never understood why. My father passed away before we could talk about it, and my mother, grieving his loss, never really talked about it.

Throughout my cooking career, I've wanted to travel internationally. I always imagined Japan would be the first place I would visit. When I enrolled in culinary school at eighteen, my first question was, "How do I make *gyoza* from scratch?"

I had never been out of the country, but my imagination was unconstrained by borders, and food would become my passport. Memories of the Koi pond in Japantown would transport me to a fish market in Tokyo. I envisioned Hong Kong whenever my chopsticks picked up a piece of Dim Sum. And I could smell the grapevines of Tuscany while kneading fresh pasta. I lived vicariously through *Great Chefs of the World* and *Samantha Brown Travels.* One day I would be traveling to these places. Eventually, I'd work in their kitchens.

Departing for Tokyo stirred many emotions: fear, excitement, nostalgia, sadness, and curiosity. I had been awarded a scholarship by the Gohan Society of New York[1], the Joyce and Helen Chen Foundation[2], and C-CAP to travel throughout Japan and China. Along with a few other chefs, I was on an adventure to experience unparalleled hospitality and to study in the presence of masters who learned from their masters. I am indebted to my dear friend, Saori Kawano, for making that trip possible. Saori is a strong Japanese woman who embraced a foreign country and worked her way to the top; she leveraged her determination and success to craft a mission to share the beauty of her culture with American chefs. Our trip was the fruit of her vision.

The Gohan Society's mission is to "advocate for a mutual appreciation of culinary heritage between the United States and Japan through outreach to chefs, culinary arts professionals, and food enthusiasts." Saori's passion and appreciation for her Japanese culture have introduced many chefs to the knowledge and beauty of Japanese cooking. Her commitment to cross-cultural education was why I was traveling to Asia.

Sitting in the Denver airport waiting for my flight, I continued practicing my basic knowledge of the Japanese language. I started again with the basics my mom had taught me: *ko-nee-chee-wah, a-rri-gato, si-or-nara.*

Japanese culture is the true definition of hospitality. Having worked in high-end hotels and restaurants all over the United States, I thought I understood what it means to entertain a guest. My travels through Japan revealed how little I knew while introducing me to new ingredients, tools, techniques, and friends.

As we arrived in Tokyo, I realized I was a foreigner—standing in the long customs line was a culture shock and a reminder of the forgotten luxuries of being a citizen. For some reason, I was highly nervous as I approached the customs officer to receive my very first passport stamp. I walked down the escalator and noticed everyone was collecting their luggage and followed suit. After going through customs, I was officially in Japan! I had made the same voyage my mom had told me about many times.

Waiting for my connecting flight to Komatsu and looking forward to meeting my fellow sojourners, all flying from New York, I enjoyed a small bowl of soba noodles from a kiosk. I smiled as I inserted the 100 yen coins into the machine. In short order, I introduced myself to Daniel Drexler of Café Boulud, Sara Bradley of Le Bernadin, and Suzanne Cupps from Untitled, and we boarded our flight to meet with Saori and her daughter, Mari. They would be our mentors in Japanese customs and culture.

In Komatsu, we were greeted by our hosts. We continued our travels via bus to the city of Yamanaka, where we checked in to a small traditional Japanese inn called a ryokan (the purpose of a ryokan is to embrace the weary traveler and extend hospitality). Having settled into our room, Daniel and I swapped traveling stories and shared our expectations for the trip. I asked about his journey to working for such a prestigious restaurant. Even though we were equals on this trip, I was in awe of his career path.

After changing into my yukata—the traditional clothing to be worn most anytime you are at the ryokan—I snapped a selfie while kneeling in front of a full-length mirror (reminiscent of the photo shared by a prior scholarship recipient, Damien Niotis). I was quickly settling in, and it was time for dinner.

Brother kneels before a mirror on his futon on his first day of experiencing Japan. The yukata is a more casual version of a traditional kimono.

Arriving at the salon for our first meal in Japan, we were greeted by our hosts, Saori and Mari, as well as our guides Michael Romano, the Chef and Culinary Director of Union Square Hospitality, and Qta Asada, a sixteenth generation restaurant owner. My first dinner in Japan was everything I could have imagined and more. We enjoyed tsukemono (pickled vegetables), local steamed rice, sashimi, miso soup, and grilled fish as we chatted about our travels and jetlag.

As the sounds of airports and busses faded and the night sky grew dark, it was time to experience the *onsen*, a traditional bathhouse—the one place on the property our yukatas were not welcome. It is only appropriate to enter the onsen showered and as naked as the day you were born. Sitting in a natural hot spring with the purest water I've ever experienced, all I could think of was, "Wow, I'm naked in Japan on my first night." I chuckled at the irony.

From kimonos to the tea service, it was the perfect introduction to Japanese cuisine. As I drifted off to sleep, I thought about the beauty and gratitude on full display in each moment. I wondered if I could, in the same way, slow down my life and enjoy every second.

Our first full day began with traditional Japanese hospitality; our breakfast table was adorned with steamed rice with shoyu kombu, miso soup, steamed omelets, and binchotan grilled Ayu fish. In America, breakfast is marked by its simplicity—the only time it ever finds favor is when it pretends to be an early lunch. But in Japan, every meal that hosts guests bursts with the formalities of traditional cuisine.

We soon began our tour of the region, meeting local suppliers, craftsmen, and artists. I marveled at the talent and traditional techniques during each stop. We learned how soy sauce is made without the intrusion of technology, watched a woodcarver live out his artistic philosophy of "using beautiful objects every day," and were inspired by a sake producer that maintains tradition while embracing his personal style.

We departed Yamanaka for Kanazawa City to begin our *stages* in different kitchens. Daniel would be working at Tsubajin, Sara at Sekitei, Suzanne at Zeniya, and I would serve first at Takitei and then at Kinjhoro. Takietei was a beautiful ryokan nestled on the upper reaches of the Sai River twenty minutes outside the city. As I arrived, I was once again transported back in time. The other chefs were done with ryokans, but I still had more to experience.

My first night working at Takitei was full of memorable moments: my favorite was receiving an invitation to have drinks and dinner with the entire restaurant team. One of the waitresses who joined us spoke a little English and became my interpreter for the evening. Having never interacted with an American chef, most were curious to learn about me and my home country. We talked about philosophies, inspirations, education, and styles of cooking.

The team took me to a small yakitori restaurant to enjoy "Japanese soul food." The dinner was full of cold beer, steamed rice, pickles, grilled chicken hearts, skewers of beef, pork, meatballs, fried chicken wings, and French fries. As we departed the restaurant, I was surprised at how American culture permeated this distant land. I immediately recognized the sounds of Teddy Riley dancing from the car radio, and one of the chefs couldn't wait to show me the rest of his American R&B collection.

The following day I had the privilege of working at Kinjhoro, a 130-year-old restaurant that maintains the highest traditions of Kaiseki cuisine. Experiencing authentic Kaiseki cuisine was life-changing. Before Japan, I had a strong appreciation for seasonal cooking and serving the best ingredients available. After working in Japan and spending time with so many professionals, I realized I was barely scratching the surface of what it meant to cook seasonally and use the best ingredients.

We toured fish and produce markets each morning, discussing

the prices and quality of some of the best ingredients I've ever seen. Afterward, we returned to the kitchen to begin the day of apprenticeship. I watched and learned. I asked questions and took notes. I learned about fermented foods, abalone liver sauce, traditional sushi, filling bento boxes, tempura, fish butchery, and, most importantly, storytelling: everything in Japan is inspired by emotion that interplays with your surroundings.

A farewell photo from the Ryokan Kinjohro culinary team. This traditional Japanese Inn is over 130 years old. Chef Brother Luck was honored to have them take this picture after working in their kitchens. (2016) Kanazawa, Japan

One of the greatest lessons I learned in Japan was to embrace nature because that's where the circle begins. On my last day of apprenticeship, the chef at Kinjhoro took me to the Kenrokuen Gardens because I had shared how I felt I understood the connection to nature. Enjoying the garden is one of the most beautiful experiences I've had in my life.

Early the following day, we departed Kanazawa City to catch the famous bullet train to Tokyo to walk with a million people through the cleanest, most organized train station I had ever been in. I was in a different world, not only thinking about America on the other side of the ocean but also the old country of Japan just a few hours away. I had immersed myself in the moment for so much of the past few days; it was a shock to return to our modern-day lifestyle and be reminded I live in the twenty-first century.

Saori had us scheduled to work with a fugu (blowfish) master that afternoon to learn the process and skill it takes to prepare the deadly fish. We watched the Ike Jime process of killing the fish humanely to preserve its quality and the intricate butchery process of crafting non-lethal pieces before enjoying numerous preparations, including sashimi, fried, and stewed. This was a once-in-a-lifetime experience I will forever cherish. Afterward, I called Tina to tell her I had survived the fugu—she didn't find my humor all that entertaining.

After a night's rest, we arrived at the Tsukiji Fish Market before the sun woke up. (We enjoyed a moment that can no longer be experienced, as we visited this famed market during its final year at its current spot before it was relocated to a newer facility a few miles away.) We received access to the tuna auction with the Shoku En representatives and watched the prized tuna sell for $10,000. Afterward, we walked through the old market and saw (but never smelled) the freshest seafood you can imagine.

The Japanese people, their culture, and their economy rely on the ocean for survival; they honor nature and life by offering nothing but the best preparations of these ingredients. I tasted uni that was other-worldly, ate sushi straight from the ocean, and learned new farming practices to further sustainability.

A rare experience of watching the auction in the historical Tsukiji Fish Market in Tokyo. This tuna fish sold for $10,000 that morning.

Inspired by all we were learning, I took notice of knives for sale in a nearby market and began searching for a left-handed *deba* knife (a thick, stout knife traditionally used in Japan for filleting fish). Saori suggested I not hurry the decision and wait until later. I discovered what later meant as we arrived at Masamoto-Sahonten just outside Kappabashi. Run by sixth-generation family member Masahiro Hirano, this is one of the best knife shops in the world.

Saori gestured to a few deba knives and smiled. I examined the remarkable craftsmanship and the fine details. I gripped the wood handle and pressed my fingers against the cold steel. I measured the weight by flicking my wrist. Just as I was deciding which of these art pieces would join me on my trip home, Saori invited our attention and said, "Please pick a knife you like. It will be my gift to you." I couldn't believe it: I was prepared to invest a few hundred dollars into the perfect knife to commemorate this trip. But Saori had arranged to have knives custom-made by Masahiro Hirano and personally engraved. My knives are beautiful, but this is one of a kind. It can never be replaced and is precisely why I don't want my cooks to touch my knives.

As we four chefs signed thank you cards and said our good-byes to our hosts, I was keenly aware of my gratitude for the people who cared about me. And not just the professional me, by the personal me. Without organizations like C-CAP or The Gohan Society, I would never have gained such an amazing opportunity to grow as a chef, a business owner, and as a person.

My experience in Japan elevated my skills to new heights. I understand hospitality in a more meaningful way. I'm much more aware of the essence of ingredients: quality, seasonality, footprint, and execution. And I discovered how vital the craftsmen, artists, fishermen, and farmers are to my cuisine.

A Dream Fulfilled

My trip to Japan was the trip of a lifetime, not only for Chef Brother Luck but also for the little boy in me. My mom's dream came true. My dream came true. And you better believe I honored my mom by spending the 100 yen coin she gave her little boy.

I've learned that I love to travel. I enjoy discovering new cultures and meeting new people. I'm tantalized by exotic and luxurious cuisines from distant lands. I've traveled to many countries since that first passport stamp: Italy, China, the Netherlands,

Mexico, and the Dominican Republic, to name a few. Every time I experience a new culture, a life lesson awaits me.

It took me thirty-three years to create an opportunity to travel internationally. Why did I wait so long?

Where do you dream of traveling to? What are you waiting for? And if it is not traveling that you desire, what is it? Do you dream of starting a business? Going back to college? Becoming an artist? Running for office? Writing your first book? What has beckoned you since childhood?

What's stopping you? Like I once did, do you feel you do not deserve any blessings in your life? Do you think dreaming is wasteful? Are you afraid to acknowledge that you are important?

I'm not offering a platitude suggesting you can achieve your dreams simply because you dreamed them. What I am saying is twofold, and they are two sides of the same coin: (1) you either need to know there are amazing people who care about you and want to help you thrive, or (2) be reminded there are some amazing people who need you to care about them because they need your help—not only to survive but to thrive. You either need to be reminded life is hard, but there is hope, or you need to be the one doing the reminding.

I'm grateful Tony Bones introduced me to not just airplanes and hotels but to the joy and learning that comes from travel. I am glad to have introduced my good friend, Dana Keith, to places he deserves to go but hadn't yet dared to walk into.

So whether it is today or ten years from now, please trust me and get lost in a new country where you don't speak the language.

21. CHILDREN JUST DON'T UNDERSTAND

A wise son brings joy to his father,
but a foolish son brings grief to his mother.

My mom was young when I was born. And having lost her husband, she was grappling to find light in the darkness, just as I was. She had two kids to care for and no family support. She was weighed down by the pressures of the same neighborhoods I grew up in. I know now what a child could never understand; my mom did the best she could.

How many of you have a perfect relationship with your parents? The saying goes that a child will learn more from who you are than from what you're trying to teach them. Over the years, I've struggled with how I feel about being my parents' child. When I look in the mirror, I see their image. My facial features resemble my mother's, but my build and hairline represent the men of my father's lineage. I'm the creation of two people who have their blood pumping through my heart every day.

Children want to make their parents proud. But how can you make someone proud if you don't understand them? I think most parents have a straightforward goal: to make their children's lives better than their own. But how do you break a cycle if that's all you know? A child's mind, like pottery, is easily molded; it will always be influenced by the decisions of the adults in their lives. My early childhood is filled with great memories and love; in my early teen years, not so much.

Tomorrow is not promised for anyone, and time waits for no one. There's no telling when you will lose your parents, but eventually, they will be gone. My pottery was shattered against the pavement on May 2, 1994.

Only a few days old, Brother Luck is held by his father and surrounded by his immediate family on Pier 39 in San Franscisco, CA. (1983)

Since the day of my father's death, I've been afraid to become a dad. I've always had this overwhelming, breath-stealing fear that if I had a kid, I would die at a young age, just as my dad did. When it comes to the idea of having children, the pain of losing a parent has plagued me like a black fog. There are various factors in my not being a dad, but this fear has loomed large for years. I'm almost forty, and there's no doe-eyed child with my smirk (or humor) looking to me for guidance.

The idea of being a parent who's not in their child's life is something I cannot fathom. Maybe it's because I had one parent taken away, and my relationship with the other was severed for years. I asked a lot of questions, but I didn't get many answers. Why don't you want me? Where did you go? What did I do wrong?

Some of you know this horrible feeling and have asked yourself these very same questions. You've experienced it firsthand. Was it a sudden death or divorce? What about an addiction that took control of you? Maybe they were incarcerated? Worst case... they abandoned you without any notice. During my childhood, it was most of the above.

My father didn't leave his family by choice, but in the coming years, I felt abandoned. The little voice inside my head screamed, "You just need to be left alone because, without him, you are alone!" The disconnect that had started with my mother quickly turned into resentment. That resentment turned into anger and defiance. I couldn't understand why she wouldn't take me to see my family. (There was strife among the adults I could never have understood then.) Still, I could hear my father's voice saying, "Listen to your mother, and don't ever disrespect her."

My mother and I regularly talked throughout my teen years, and I learned she was struggling with her own life. After a bad breakup, she floated aimlessly and found comfort in old habits. I distanced myself because I didn't want to be part of that lifestyle anymore, but I had inner angst.

Shortly after Tina and I got married, my mom reached out to ask if she could stay with us; I never hesitated. She had moved to Louisiana for a short stint only to return to Phoenix. I had no idea how far she had fallen. Within the first few days, I asked her to leave because I couldn't tolerate her disrespecting Tina or me. The streets of her past haunted her steps no matter how fast she ran.

And when she tried to escape the pain, she kept tripping. I don't remember wanting to help, but I don't think she would have accepted, even if I did.

A few months had gone by since the last time I'd last seen my mom. The dinner reservation was at six o'clock, and Tina and I were about to meet her. It didn't go well the last time we talked. I had asked her to move out, and she left with both guns blazing. Ironically, we were eating at a place called My Mother's Restaurant on 19th Avenue in West Phoenix. As we walked toward the back of the restaurant, I heard a familiar voice say, "Hey, you two, over here!"

I looked at this stranger who was beckoning Tina and me. When I made eye contact, my heart skipped a beat. This was no stranger. This was my mom. She had lost so much weight that I didn't recognize her. She looked frail. The last few months had not been kind. The only thing I recognized besides her voice was her crystal blue eyes. My apprehension must have been felt by Tina because she nudged me toward the table. We sat and talked for a few hours, but I could not tell you the context. I cried the entire car ride home because I believed deep in my soul I was about to lose another parent.

Death or jail. Those are the only two options you have when you're an addict. My brother is still weighing those options.

My mother was lucky. She was given a second chance at life. Her story is fascinating, but it is her story to tell. I'm very proud of the woman she has become. The relationship we have today is not the one I knew twenty years ago. And I am grateful she and Tina have a loving relationship today as well.

Everyone has a past. Some of our pasts are filled with things they are not proud of. The shame accompanying that luggage is heavy. I'm talking about repacking your bags at the airline counter heavy. I've had shame in my story. I've done things I'm not proud of. I've hurt people, but I'm pretty sure you have too. There is no such thing as perfection. Only the idea of perfection exists, which means attaining it is impossible. So why do we judge others so harshly for their past mistakes? Why can't we forgive? We don't have to forget, but it takes tremendous energy to carry that weight.

Life has a way of turning everything upside down without notice. One minute you can be on top of the world: big home, fancy cars, money in the bank—but the next, it's gone. You've lost the job you worked so hard for. You can't afford to pay the mounting bills. The things you treasure most are repossessed. Child protective services have removed your children from the house. You're left with nothing. You're truly alone.

I've watched my fair share of people lose everything. Some are in jail. Others are homeless. Many are dead. The common denominator is often some form of addiction. Talking to someone who thinks their only option to the pain is the bottle, a needle, or the pipe can feel hopeless, but remember, you cannot help an addict until they want to help themselves.

It took years and small steps to rebuild the relationship I have with my mom. When she wasn't in my life, it felt easier. Out of sight, out of mind, right? When she decided to move to Colorado a few years ago, I didn't expect what it would trigger for me emotionally. There were so many festering wounds and unspoken words I just shoved it all into a closet. Carlos Whitaker writes in his book *Kill the Spider* that we all have spiders in our closets. And what's the first thing you do when you walk into a closet and feel a spider web as it covers your face? Survey says: immediately scream while flailing your arms. The next step is to hightail it faster than Usain Bolt and slam the door shut. But what happens the next time you walk back into that closet? Those same webs will still be there. It's because you never killed the spider that created them. I had never killed my spiders. They were shooting webs everywhere as if Spiderman was finally retiring, and there'd be an audition to take his place. If the spider is the root of the problem, then their webs are the stories you recall about that issue. It's important to remember there are two sides to every story. Have you heard the other version?

When I came off *Top Chef* the first time, my mother was very upset with me. I could tell she wasn't happy, but I didn't know why. She told me it wasn't my place to put her business on the street as I did. There were things about her past that she had not shared with the people in her new life. I felt awful. I had made the mistake of assuming because it was a part of my story, I was free and clear to discuss it. A relationship requires two people. You must be aware of your actions and how they will affect the other people in your life. The decisions I made to disclose my past affected more than just me.

I asked my mother to join me for lunch, and we had one of the deepest conversations we had ever embarked on. She was ready to talk, and so was I. We discussed my journey through therapy and how her generation fears being labeled and rarely seeks help. I shared stories about my childhood she didn't know. She gave me clarity on stories I thought I knew about our past. The two of us bonded that day and have continued to talk ever since.

I'm very close with my mom and cherish every second with her. I've learned so much about her, and I'm now willing to ask even more questions. I can have a mature conversation and see the perspective from her lens instead of my childlike selfishness.

It took me years to realize the trauma of her story and how it affected her. She is one of the toughest people I know, and it's hard to imagine how she's overcome the obstacles she's faced in life. I love my mom and am saddened by how much time we missed over the years.

When you're frustrated with the decisions or choices of your parents, I encourage you to stop and ask yourself one question: What are they going through? Sometimes we forget our parents are also the children of their parents. They have a story that's just as important as yours.

Can you look at your parent's side of the story and listen as an adult instead of a child? I guarantee you: their lives were hard too. But if you are willing to forgive, there is a bit of hope.

22. BLOODLINE

Do not withhold good from those to whom it is due,
when it is in your power to act.

My brother, Slade, and I are only three years apart but have always lived on opposite ends of the spectrum; if my demeanor is cool and collected, his is wild and unpredictable. Growing up in San Francisco, he earned the nickname *Monster* because he was always scaring whoever was babysitting him. He was the child who had no fear and thrived in pushing boundaries as far as possible. My brother embraced the rage of life and had no concerns about safety or precaution.

When our father died, Slade was only seven years old. He never learned about respect, humility, strength, and passion from Dad. We were thrust into a world with no real rules. The safety nets were burned down, and both of us were pushed off the cliff. We had to depend on each other to survive the cruel realities waiting for us once we landed.

I love my brother, and only he can tell our story the way it happened because he was there for most of it: He knows the neglect and abuse. He remembers the loneliness. He knows what it feels like to grow up too fast. Slade learned to cope in a different way than I did. As I built walls to protect myself, he expressed anger to keep people away. We both lived with a survivalist mentality and fought every day to make it. Within a few years, we were both hardened street kids who had learned to strike first when someone came at us.

Slade went to jail for the first time when he was eleven years old. He had punched a teacher in the face for disrespecting him. My best friend Garret and I were sitting in the living room when he came sprinting through the door and ran out to the backyard. We both got up to see what was going on and found him hiding under the house.

"The police are chasing me for hitting a teacher. I just ran home when I realized I had messed up. Don't tell them I'm here," he whispered through the plywood.

The police officers showed up a few minutes later and asked if we had seen him. I doubt they believed our response, but I wasn't letting them past the front door. Slade was arrested the next day and sent to juvenile hall. Over the next six years, he would be in and out of correctional facilities leaving me on my own to fend for myself.

I can only imagine the horrors he endured during his childhood living in juvenile hall. I would drive up to see him regularly, and we would sit in the visitor's room playing dominoes until his time was up. During one visit, he asked if he could wear my new *North Carolina Tar Heels* jacket so he could feel more normal as we played bones. I was a little surprised by his request as he seemed to be hardening on the inside and was carrying an edge of anger and strength: his desire to "be normal" didn't align with his "don't mess with me" attitude.

Slade was released a few months after Tina and I started dating, and he came home with some new muscles. I had just turned seventeen, and he was almost fourteen. As brothers often do (at least those I grew up with), we argued about something stupid, and then we threw punches. I'll never forget his stare and subsequent threat as he recoiled from a right hook that struck him square in the jaw. "Hit me again; that shit doesn't do anything but make me tougher." I quickly realized Slade was no longer my cartoon-watching little brother. He no longer looked up to me. He was now a young man (or an old boy?) who wasn't taking shit from anyone. His time in juvie had changed him, and now he was back home living with our mom. It was just the three of us and her boyfriend, but I knew I had to get out. Life at home was not conducive to my new relationship with Tina or my desire to finish school and begin my culinary career. Within the next year, I was helping them pack up a moving truck headed to Louisiana. I was staying in Phoenix to attend college on a scholarship. I cried as they drove away. They were tears of shame and relief; I knew I had given up on trying to take care of the remaining two family members in my life.

While in Louisiana, Slade began cooking at a restaurant named Copelands; I was so proud of him. He would call me to talk about the ingredients on the sauté station or how busy last night's service had been. I loved reconnecting with him (food really does bring families together). Tina and I had just eloped, and I had earned the title of sous chef for the Hyatt Regency Phoenix. As Slade and I shared battle stories from our respective kitchens, my mind ran wild, envisioning us side-by-side in a restaurant. I could hear my father bragging about his two boys who became chefs. I've always dreamed about running a restau-rant with my brother, but as they say, anytime you want to hear God laugh, just tell him your plans.

My brother ended up getting married while in Louisiana. He had met a woman with children and wanted to provide. He joined the army and was soon shipped off to basic training in Georgia. I remember looking at a photo he sent me—one in which he was wearing camo and holding an M-16 rifle—and thinking, "Holy shit, not only is this kidded ripped, but now is learning how to use deadly weapons!"

Shortly after my transfer to San Antonio, Texas, Slade was getting ready for his Advanced Individual Training, which followed boot camp. Wanting to see him and also take possession of our father's ashes while he was away, we met in New Orleans to spend a week catching up. I shared all about my new life with Tina, my cooking career, and how hard I was working at the new property in Texas. He told me all about his life and adventures in the military. At one point, as we were talking about the future, he turned and said, "After AIT, my job title is going to be 92 Golf."

"What the heck is that?" I inquired.

He smirked and said, "I'm going to be a cook in the army. Funny huh? There are still two chefs in the family."

Since my brother's military career, he's had a tough time finding his way. It seems no matter how hard I try, my wisdom and life experience aren't enough to save him. I don't know all the details of what he endured during and after his military career, but he is not the same man I laughed with and loved during that trip to New Orleans. He has his story, and I have mine; and whenever possible, when our lives intersect, it is bittersweet.

Slade and Brother Luck in New Orleans, LA. (2005)

When I opened *Four by Brother Luck* in Colorado Springs, I received some profound insight and counsel from Marcus Samuelsson: "A restaurant comes from the term to restore. A restaurant needs to be constantly restoring the community and its people. If you're not engaged in the community, you will never be successful in your city."

Today, I invest a significant amount of time and energy working with the 92 Golfs (culinary specialists) out of Fort Carson in Colorado Springs. In conjunction with the command at Fort Carson, we created Bridging the Gap, a program to emphasize the relationship between civilians and soldiers. During the program, the 92 Golfs spend forty-five days with me learning various culinary, professional, and financial aspects of the hospitality industry. We develop their skills inside and outside the kitchen by teaching them personal communication skills, best entrepreneurship practices, management theory, marketing strategy, and the value of intention. We empower them to succeed as business leaders and community influencers during and after their military careers.

During the pandemic, I wanted to stay connected to people, so with my friend Dana Keith's expertise and support, we created the #NoLucksGiven podcast[1] to talk with culinary professionals, learn from leaders, and encourage as many people as possible. As it pertains to mentorship, leadership, and caring for others, one of the most influential podcasts was our panel discussion with army leaders from Fort Carson: Lieutenant Colonel Mike Olsen, Captain Josh Trinkle, First Sergeant Jason Marshall, and Sergeant First Class Alex Phillips.

Learning from each other during the one-hour discussion, we recognized mentors come in various forms: moms and dads, family, friends, older kids in the neighborhood, coworkers, faith leaders, scout leaders, coaches, teachers, and more.

And we collected valuable axioms about leadership.

- You don't know who is watching you.
- There are good mentors, and there are bad mentors.
- The best mentors support you while simultaneously challenging you.
- The strongest leaders excel at following.
- Great leaders empower people and create systems to help them succeed.
- Each person has a unique story and must be cared for as an individual.
- Practical leadership is acting the way you want your followers to act.
- Make every effort to ensure your team understands why you do what you do.
- Establish, communicate, and maintain standards.
- Make your leadership about the success of others.
- Be willing to sacrifice for those you lead.
- Don't let your fear of failure stop you from trying.

Having employed hundreds, if not thousands of people in my various restaurants in the last ten years, I can say people will never cease to disappoint you, and people will never cease to amaze you. And every one of them is worth your sacrifice.

I'm thankful for the leadership at Fort Carson and their partnership in Bridging the Gap. Though I cannot help my brother with his direction in life today, I know I can honor and serve other soldiers. I want to be a good mentor and an even better friend to them. I know life is hard, but I also know there is hope.

23. MENTORSHIP

Listen to my instruction and be wise; do not disregard it.

What is a mentor? By definition, a mentor is "someone who teaches or gives help and advice to a less experienced and often younger person."[1] So why does mentorship matter so much, especially to me? It comes down to six words in that definition: *someone who teaches or gives help.*

Many people in my life became my mentors: most were good; a few were terrible. Both types fit the description of being a mentor—there's no directive about ethics.

As lifelong students, we are meant to realize our own life lessons, hopefully, to be protected from the harshest lessons by those who can protect us. As lifelong teachers, we must be willing to be transparent and vulnerable to help others through their difficult seasons. But in the end, we all need to learn who we are—our true identity—and believe it and trust it. One of the keys to life is that we are meant to live it together. Indulge me, if you will, as I share a couple of stories about people in my life.

I met Dana Keith a few years ago while at one of my previous restaurants. His sister had been my sous chef and suggested we meet.

What stood out to me about Dana was what he did with the money after I paid him; he cashed his check and invested in more camera equipment.

Whenever I'm deciding on working with someone, there's one thing that matters most to me: are they willing to do the work? It is easy for someone to talk about what they want to achieve. It's an entirely different discussion when push comes to shove.

How badly do they want it? What are they willing to do for it? Are they invested in themselves? Have they committed to their dreams? Whenever I choose to invest myself in someone, it's because I see that spark.

Dana's drive to become a filmmaker kept me engaged as a mentor. We talked about his business structure and how to handle taxes. We discussed how beautiful life can be and how our doubts and insecurities keep us from living.

Every time we worked together, he purchased more equipment: Eventually, his boom mic became official—no more duct-taped broom handles. His wireless mics capture better quality audio.

He proudly flew his new drone camera while we were filming in New York (and almost got arrested for doing so). We launched a podcast together.

And the result? We became friends.

Isn't this what real mentorship should be about? Building trust. Becoming friends. Helping one another. Finding enough confidence in yourself to not make it about you? Selflessness comes with mentorship. When you do it right, it never stops.

I'm grateful that Marcus Samuelsson has always been selfless in guiding and mentoring me, and tonight would be another night that I would get to spend some time with him.

As I donned my blue pinstriped suit jacket, which caused my light pink dress shirt to pop, I was thinking about the first time I stood side-by-side with Chef Marcus Samuelsson nearly fifteen years earlier when I was in my early twenties. I tucked my pink and blue pocket square into the left side of my chest. The slim-fit blue jeans were creased sharp. I loved the royal blue corduroy sneakers with the tan bottoms, which complemented my outfit! I would once again be standing next to Marcus—this time at a C-CAP charity event.

"How do you think this outfit will compare to Marcus'?" I asked Tina.

Marcus Samuelsson always looks stylish wherever he goes. I've been watching him for many years, and there's been a shift in his appearance. He no longer dons the blue chef coat with gold embroidery—that was the young chef I knew from the past—he has become a fashion icon. His brightly colored outfits are usually accompanied by a signature brim hat.

"I want to make sure I stand out just as he does," I continued telling Tina.

We were in Manhattan. You know, the big apple, a place where dreams are made. The skyscrapers and neon lights screamed inspiration. Tina and I were attending the thirtieth anniversary of C-CAP Changing Lives, a national benefit dinner hosted along the choppy waters of Chelsea Piers.

Upon our entry we were immediately greeted by Marcus Samuelsson; he was being followed by a full camera crew recording his every movement throughout the crowded room.

Damn, he looked sharp. Marcus had on a blue suit complemented with shorts, multi-colored sneakers, and his signature hat.
I guess there's no topping the master at work. How ironic that I've
gone from admiring and mimicking his cooking style to chasing
his presence!

Marcus Samuelsson and Brother Luck filming in New York City at the C-CAP
Benefit dinner. (2022) Tina Luck

"Good to see you. I love the sober week thing you did for your employees. You're thinking outside the box. That's what it's about," Marcus affirmed.

"I just want this next generation of restaurant people to consider healthier lifestyle choices," I explained before the camera crew chased him as he stepped away to greet another guest.

The evening was a celebration of the work C-CAP had been doing for decades. The attendees varied: organizations executives, C-CAP mentors, and former and current C-CAP students. While the food was amazing and the presentation was inspiring, the conversation got as real as it could get when talking to some young high school students.

"So, what's your salary?" a young girl asked me.

I chuckled. She had yet to learn money would never be the solution and, most likely, whatever she was running from would continue to follow her wherever she went. That is until someone pauses and acts as a signpost telling her the way she should go.

"I own my businesses now. There's no limit to how much money I can earn in a day. I no longer allow someone to tell me how much I'm worth an hour."

Work is noble. It is first and foremost about the people we serve. And, yes, it is also about the money. But we need to stop letting the world define us by our material wealth and start embracing the truth of who we intrinsically are.

Mentorship requires an awareness of your student's reality. What are they going through? How does their background affect their decision-making? What motivates them? What infuriates them? If they become defensive, how can you scale those walls?

As I've grown in my career, I regularly ask myself: How do I create for others what I didn't have coming up? When I was younger, I was invigorated by the idea of working with celebrity chefs who were in magazines or on television, but it was rare to meet them. Today I host and participate in many celebrity chef dinners. When doing so, there's nothing more rewarding than watching my team interact with the people they've watched on television or followed on Instagram. I remember that feeling. Watching my chef de cuisine, Ashley, get to work with legends like Tanya Holland was moving. She was so excited to speak with a woman who has overcome adversity in a male-dominated industry. That Joe Flamm taught my sauté cooks how to make his pasta dough from scratch is invaluable. Having Chris Scott teach his famous biscuit recipe to my entire crew was beautiful. Knowing Silvia Barban was willing to share her authentic Italian focaccia recipe with my pastry chef is what it's all about.

Brother and Tina Luck on the opening night of Four by Brother Luck in downtown Colorado Springs. (2017) Brian Lewis

I acknowledge—by the support and efforts of my mentors—I have become one of those admired chefs. More importantly, because of them, I'm teaching and helping young cooks, creating experiences today that will become their memories tomorrow. Whom will you be inspiring in twenty years?

My team is everything. The people I interact with daily inspire me. They come from all walks of life. Homelessness. Domestic Violence. Poverty. Incarceration. Immigration. Neglect. The list goes on and on. I get to inspire people who have a similar story to my own. Young men who lack guidance. Strong women with ideas and confidence. People of color. Some of whom struggle with disabilities. Others who are embracing identity. Or many like myself who struggle with their mental health.

It's not your job to make other people successful. Your job is to inspire and motivate others so they can elevate to the next level. Any person chasing a dream needs to want it. They need to trudge through their own mud. But they need you to teach, help, and advise them.

You can't help someone become successful. They have to define what success means for themselves. But I will say: It's not money, fame, power, celebrity status, or followers that matter—it's people.

While most people reading this book know me as Chef Brother Luck, I'm just a man whose parents named him Brother. While the title is still important, it is no longer my identity. After nearly forty years, I've defined my life's priorities: faith, family, and food. It is about my relationship with God. It is about my family, friends, and team members. It is about my passion for food. In. That. Order. I screw up the order every day, but I still try.

Because of my growing compassion for people, I've become an advocate for mental health. Why? Because we need each other.

There's no shame in admitting I have struggled. At times, as you are about to learn in reading the next chapter, it has been especially dark. I'm learning to be vulnerable, and as scary as it is, it's worth it because you are worth it. And when you share your pain with me, it doesn't push me away; it draws me toward you.

24. WHISKEY LULLABY

Whoever isolates himself seeks his own desire;
he breaks out against all sound judgment.

I tried to kill myself while filming my second season of *Top Chef*. I was so tired of not being good enough that despair deceived me into giving up. As I sat on the hotel bed, I concluded: It's over. All I do is let people down, especially the ones I love the most. Everyone who believed in me will have to watch me lose again on national television. Why do I keep doing this to myself? Why am I even here? I shouldn't have left Tina!

My sorrow bombarded me: I'm too weak. I've always been weak. I was never good enough to be here. Why do I lie to myself thinking I'm even a little bit talented? Why don't I look in the mirror and tell myself that I'm ready to give up? I could end all this pain and suffering tonight!

I looked at the six-foot, wall-mounted mirror next to my bed and began to cry as I made eye contact with myself. My demons were right. I had been lying to myself, and I finally felt convinced of the lies I had been telling. I mouthed six words to myself in the mirror as it resonated over and over in my brain: You should just end the pain.

I took another swallow from the bottle of Bulleit Rye, which was my only companion that night. I was drunk and had no intentions of stopping. I decided my finish line would be to blackout—then I'd feel completely numb. I didn't want to feel anything anymore. Feeling the pain of berating myself for the last few hours, my eyes hurt from the tears.

I was on day three of being sequestered in a hotel room that I had come to despise; I raged with hate, most of it directed at myself. While filming a series of episodes, once a contestant's pursuit of victory fails, they are sequestered and instructed to remain in isolation—often in a hotel room. (The whole point is to maintain the integrity of the viewer's entertainment experience by keeping you from spilling the beans about what's happening during production. Plus, you'll need to repeatedly return to the set to perform pickup lines or contribute to edits.) It is a lonely, grievous time of solitude that feeds doubt and elevates insecurities. With too much time to think, I felt like I was a child sent to his room to think about what I had done.

I lay there thinking about my beautiful wife, Tina. She was the only reason I had for living. I had let her down when I walked out the door to fly to Kentucky for a second chance at fame. I knew my actions revealed where she stood in my priorities. In my self-ishness, I had hurt her, and the damage would take years to repair.

She knew what this experience had done to me the first time. *Top Chef* season fifteen in Colorado had been emotionally scarring; I'd become mentally fragile. I kept telling myself I was in Kentucky to prove a point: I should have won the first time. But who was I fooling? I knew the real truth: I was chasing validation and approval. I was grossly insecure and didn't feel good enough. I wasn't good enough as a husband. I wasn't good enough as a chef. I especially wasn't good enough for myself. I deeply regretted leaving the one person on earth who believed in me. I had deserted Tina when she needed me the most, and I was too ashamed to go home.

I took another sleeping pill. The bottle tipped as I continued to drink the remaining bit of whiskey—empty bottles were strewn across the floor. The whiskey and sleep medicine comforted me. I was ready to see my father again; his voice would soothe my pain. I thought about my wife's beautiful face and gentle voice as I drifted off into the abyss. Chef Brother Luck had become the worst enemy of Brother Luck, and the shame of another defeat was killing the man. I gave up that night.

An Awakening

I woke up to the sounds of news anchors discussing the morning's current events. My television was still on from the night before. The babble slowly woke me from my drunken stupor. I blinked a few times, rubbed my eyes, and tried to make sense of the fog in which I was lost. I began to weep as I remembered my desperation from just a few hours before. I recalled the feel of the glass bottle touching my lips and the bitter taste of the pills as I sought to end my pain. As I rolled over and hugged my pillow, with clarity that wasn't perfectly sober, I couldn't breathe. I tried to kill myself last night. I intended to alleviate my pain and end my shame once and for all. But somehow, having gone to sleep, I forgot to die.

Suddenly, the words from the news show pierced the fog: "Anthony Bourdain, accomplished chef and media personality, was found dead in his hotel room last night."

What? I reached over to the side table to grab the remote. I turned up the volume. "The celebrity chef was found unconscious in his hotel room. He was discovered unresponsive by his colleagues this morning."

As I continued listening, I watched the corresponding news ticker crawl across the screen. I felt like Mike Tyson had just punched me in the chest. I'd been battling the similar demons last night. How had I survived, but he did not? Like me, he was battling depression. But he did not survive to see the sunrise. He fell to an enemy who knew how to isolate him. His demons slaughtered his common sense. I do not doubt he felt alone—as with all who are beleaguered by depression. We had been telling ourselves the same lie. But God.

I had escaped an impossible situation and would live to tell the tale. God had given me a second chance. Deep in my soul, I know how lucky I am. I cannot explain why others are not. But what I do know is an enemy will always try to isolate his prey, creating an easier target. If no one is there to watch your back, you're vulnerable. Just as I was. Just at Anthony was.

I didn't know Anthony Bourdain personally, but I connected with him emotionally and professionally. Early in my career, I felt connected to his journey. When I first read *Kitchen Confidential*, there was a familiarity in his words. His culinary insights and storytelling filtered my view of the world. I had eaten his food at Les Halles (those are some damn good fries). I had worked with many of the chefs he had. My interviews shared similar insecurities.

Waking up to the news of his death shocked life back into me. It was surreal. What if it had been me? Would they have broadcast my story on national television? "A *Top Chef* contestant commits suicide during filming!" Would anyone miss me?

I know the aftermath of suicide. I know the feeling of asking questions and never getting answers. I know the pain and anger. Why did they do it? Could we have done more? I'm so sad and hurt. I'm pissed off they did that to all of us. Why would I even consider doing that to people I love? I'm filled with shame and regret as I type this.

I made a decision that morning, and every day I remind myself of it. As I stood barefoot on the cold tile of the bathroom floor and washed the shame off my face, crying the entire time but grateful to be alive, I decided I wanted to live.

With the announcement of Top Chef Colorado *came its contenders. Brother Luck poses for his profile picture. (2017) Getty Images*

I achieved fame. I traveled the world. I made more money than my parents hoped I would. I found love from an amazing woman, and her family made me one of their own. But none of it was enough because it was never about cooking, fame, leisure, money, or even love. It was and is about the truth of who I am—who God created me to be. While I thought I learned the lesson in a hospital room in Arizona, it was a long and lonely night and a sun-filled morning in a hotel room in Kentucky that changed everything.

For those of us who struggle with depression, anxiety, loneliness, fear, worry, doubt, addiction, or any other pain that seeks to destroy us, we need to seek help. As I mentioned earlier in this book, when I was a teenager, I hated the idea of seeing a counselor. But as an adult, the process of being vulnerable with a trusted counselor has been healing for me. Please, if you have an enemy who is isolating you from your family, friends, and everyone else who cares about you, don't continue to fight alone. You don't have to be the strong one today. Let the people who love you—those who have your back—stand and fight with you.

We all need to understand: Crying is not a sign of weakness. A therapist is not the enemy. Hiding your pain will only cause more. Don't embrace loneliness; that is not your friend.

I have grown to like who I am. More importantly, I smile when I think about whom I am becoming.

Whom do you see in the mirror? Do you like that person? Can you love who you are? There is only one you. Do not be afraid to embrace that love. It's time to say it out loud—I love myself!

My memories of waking up in a Kentucky hotel room will always be a reminder to me: God has a plan for my life. Yes, I still have questions and doubts: Who am I? What's my purpose on this earth? Am I deserving of love? Why should I keep on trying? But now I have more answers, and by God's grace, I will never give up.

25. ROOM SERVICE

He who finds a wife finds what is good
and receives favor from the LORD.

There's a rush of serotonin making you feel alive when you are included in something important and meaningful to you.

"You would be a great addition to the cast for this TV show!"
"We would like to cordially invite you to..."
"Are you interested in flying to...?"

For years, I said yes to nearly any and everything because: "It is about damn time they notice how awesome I am!" said the sixteen-year-old in me. Then I started to say yes because I was finally getting the recognition I was earning through my pride, courage, perseverance, and determination.

Nowadays, these messages are more common than they once were. And it still feels great! And I want to do everything! But at what cost? I've learned every yes is balanced with a no, and some of them even require a sacrifice. One of the key identifiers of maturing is a willingness to delay gratification. I did not do that well as a child or as a young man. I wanted what I wanted, and I wanted it now! With time, I've learned to ask questions when opportunities arise: Do I want to do it because it feels good? Am I afraid of being left out? What will I have to stop doing to make it happen? Will anyone be negatively impacted if I do it?

Since being on Bravo's *Top Chef*, I've declined numerous invitations to participate in television shows. Why? I can guarantee it is not a result of the same youthful arrogance that once rebuffed Guy Fieri. Instead, I know who I am and am satisfied with who I am becoming. I'm no longer willing to say yes to any and everything and jeopardize my priorities: faith, family, and food.

In the summer of 2021, I was invited to participate in the Aspen Food and Wine Festival, which I believe is the most prestigious food festival of the year. As a successful professional chef, I dreamed of attending this cooking event alongside the mentors I shadowed so many years ago.

In doing so, I would be considered an equal—perhaps the most satisfactory accomplishment of my career. The team at Woody Creek Distillery, a local Colorado brand, requested I represent their brand at the festival. (Famed actor, William H. Macy, was their brand ambassador, and I would get the opportunity to work with him.)

I was honored. My brain boiled over with ideas as I planned my dishes.

My Father's Dirty Rice infused
with Green Apple Pico de Gallo
&
Triple M Bar Smoked Lamb
with Bow and Arrow Farms Blue Grits

Tina and Brother Luck at the Aspen Food & Wine Festival. (2018)

Having served 3,000 dishes over two days, my time cooking at the festival was over. I was proud of what we presented to our guests. Breaking down my station, I smiled at my assistant chef, Ashley Brown, and started singing, "Cause I've got a golden ticket" from Willy Wonka.

She laughed out loud as she wrapped the leftovers in plastic film. I held up the guest pass my friend and *Top Chef* colleague Byron Gomez secured for me.

"I can only get one chef, but here you go. I'll see you later at the top of the mountain," he said.

The ticket was my passport to the Top of the Mountain party where the slope-side gondola replaced limousines—every celebrity chef would be attending. It was an invite-only event. With Covid-19 concerns still looming, occupancy was restricted. It was Cinderella's ball.

After passing through security, I stepped into my carriage, which lifted me to 10,900 feet. After nearly fourteen minutes, while my head was in the clouds, my feet were firmly back on solid ground, walking toward the Cloud Nine Alpine Bistro. I had only been up there once before: when we were filming the finale episode of *Top Chef* Colorado. We, the eliminated contestants, stood outside, shivering in the wind, waiting to learn who would be crowned the season fifteen winner. I only stepped inside long enough to watch Joe Flamm receive his crown.

I immediately began looking for familiar faces; I had worked with many of them over the last few years. A bit sheepish, with the safety and anonymity of my carriage behind me, I walked toward the groups of attendees gathered under a string of lights illuminating the courtyard. I recognized a few people, smiled, and kept looking for a stronghold to step into. When I noticed Marcus Samuelsson, I knew I had found my place.

He greeted me with the strongest gesture of love: we connected hands and embraced in a brief hug. "How you doing?" Marcus inquired. "It's good to see you."

"I don't feel like I belong here. There are so many high-profile celebrities here," I confessed.

Guy Fieri walked by, and I became even more uncomfortable.

"I have no idea why I was even invited," I mumbled. My insecurities were at an all-time high and on full display. My palms were sweating. The toes of my shoes danced around on the pavement. I picked up my head and looked at Marcus. He got quiet and looked me directly in the eye.

"Look around. You're on the top of a mountain with all of us. You've made it. Regardless of how differently we've all climbed this mountain, everyone here has made it to the top. Your story is important. How you got here is even more critical. There are so many young chefs out there who need to hear how Brother Luck made it to the top of this mountain."

Marcus' assurance soothed my insecurities and bolstered my confidence. None of our journeys are identical. Each of us is striving toward something meaningful. We all deserve to be valued and invited. None of us need to climb the mountain alone.

In my early days, I had a track record of circling the base of many mountains—afraid to risk the climb. But on that night, having once again laced my boots, I trudged to the top of my Mount Everest and grabbed hold of the rope connected to my Sherpa in front of me. With a little bit of frostbite and a whole lot of fatigue, I caught a glimpse of the sun cresting the peak.

I asked Marcus if he was still interested in writing the introduction to my book. He happily obliged. "I'd be honored to write the introduction. I need to keep floating around and continue saying hello to some people. You have a good time tonight." Marcus departed into the reception as I picked my head up and walked in behind him.

I strolled away from the courtyard into the party and noticed someone I had become a big fan of—Kat Kinsman, the food editor for *Food and Wine* magazine. In addition to being remarkable at her craft, she is an advocate for mental health. We were supposed to speak together on stage in San Diego the year prior, but the pandemic had canceled the event. I had read so many of her articles and knew her social media posts intimately. After a brief internal discussion about whether to interrupt her conversation, I mustered the confidence to introduce myself: "Good evening Kat. I'm Brother Luck. I'm a big fan of your work."

She paused and smiled before replying: "It's nice to finally meet you, Brother Luck. I'm a big fan of your message. I cannot wait to interview you to hear more. Do you have time over the next few days in Aspen to chat?"

Kat had seen my essay written for the James Beard Foundation. She was aware of my vulnerability within the social media world. Her enthusiastic and powerful words were unexpectedly confirming my aspirations to become a writer and thought leader serving those whose lives are unpredictably hard. I have a passion for helping people through their struggles, especially those working in the culinary world, and she shared my enthusiasm!

Affirmed for the second time in just a few minutes (not because of my food but because of who I am and the message of hope I share with people), I walked into the party with my smiling face. I greeted many of my colleagues: Katsuji Tanabe, Claudette Zepeda, Karen Akunowicz, Dawn Wilson, Shota Nakajima, Joe Flamm, Stephanie Izard, Brooke Williamson, Byron Gomez. We all shared an experience that catapulted us into stardom.

Celebrity chefs gather and celebrate at the Aspen Food and Wine Festival. A handful of Top Chefs pose for this cameo appearance. Back row: Byron Gomez, Brother Luck, Katsuji Tanabe, and Joe Flamm. Front row: Claudette Zepeda and Stephanie Izard. (2021) Galdones Photography

As the evening progressed and I finished my Negroni, it suddenly hit me: Tina was at the hotel and not by my side. What was I doing here? As great as it was, the party fell short of my expectations because the person I loved the most was not here to share it with me.

With the string lights to my back, I boarded the gondola, departing for the base of the mountain. My head swirled during the fourteen minutes down as I once again considered my priorities: faith, family, and food. With Tina alone in a hotel room, had I again chosen my career instead of her?

Too late for private cars, and with my hotel room in Snowmass, I took a seat on a bench at the bus station. Just minutes before, I had been sipping champagne and eating caviar. Now I was a kid again, riding public transportation and trying to find my way home. After an hour of bus rides, I walked into my hotel and pressed the fifth-floor button harder than I should have. I scanned my key card to the room door and breathed a sigh of relief. It was one o'clock in the morning. Tina was awake and nestled in the giant comforter of our king-size bed.

"How was the party?" she asked.

"I realized none of this matters unless I'm with you," I replied.

"Are you hungry? There's some leftover bolognese and chicken tenders on the counter from room service," she offered through her smile.

"Absolutely. I'm starving."

One of the best meals of my life was that night's room-service bolognese and cold chicken tenders.

Regardless of what you achieve in your life, how much money you make, or the credentials you earn, it is all meaningless if you lose the people who help you pick your head up.

Don't chase validation: You already matter. You're amazing. You're one of a kind.

Don't trust the loneliness. Fight for your family. Run toward your friends. Don't make it easy for your enemy to pick you off.

Don't be afraid to get hurt. Take a chance on people. Climb a mountain. Share your story.

That night in Snowmass Village, God revealed a page of his master plan to me—one I will remember for the rest of my life—without love, nothing else matters.

Life is hard. But God.

EPILOGUE: A MENTAL PAUSE
BUTTON

On March 16, 2020, I was forced to suspend operations of my restaurants due to the government's reaction to the Covid-19 pandemic—all restaurants were to suspend all indoor operations. What the heck did that mean? I had no game plan; there were no industry guidelines for this. I assumed it was all some scare and would blow over.

Following a virtual staff meeting, I told my fifty employees there was no more work. We couldn't open our restaurants. I would do everything I could to support them, but I didn't know what to do. I took to social media and vented my feelings:

March 17, 2020
   You know I'm not gonna lie, man. Last night was an emotional night; I broke down. I couldn't. Having to lay that many people off for something we didn't even do was just wrong. My wife and I sat there in tears. You know we own our businesses. We're small business owners. We've worked hard to get to this point. We fight for every crumb, and we fight for every employee. To have something like this happen, and we understand the safety of people, but

there's no plan of action. There's no solution put in place. How do we take care of these families? How do we take care of these businesses?

That's where we must start. I refuse to give up. Fuck that, and I'm sorry for my language, but fuck that. We're going to fight. You know we're going to fight. We're going to fight by utilizing our community because the outreach that I got last night from all of you encouraged me and reminded me of what perseverance, determination, and courage means. We're going to be opening our curbside tomorrow. It's going to be some fun menu items for individuals or group meals for the family. We're also going to be doing some favorite dishes off the menu.

But I want you to come down and check us out because what's most important about that is whatever you decide to pay is going directly to the staff. That's who we need to protect. This isn't about profits right now. It's about protecting the people who don't' have any dollars saved up. The people who live check to check. The people who all lost their jobs yesterday. Its' not right. We've got to make that right.

We've got to make that right as a community. Any food leftover will be taken down to the soup kitchen to feed those in need. If it's on the shelves, then I don't want anything going bad when people are hungry and in need.

At the end of the day, I'm a chef. I cook food. I cook great food. My team cooks great food. We will not be focusing on one specific cuisine or style of food. What we're going to be doing is taking care of you. You hit us up. What do you need? Are you gluten-free? Paleo? Do you have Dietary Restrictions? We can cook any of those requests. We're going to move forward by making this about the community. I love you, Colorado Springs. I know you're going to rock with us. My heart, you all filled it yesterday. But let's take care of our people. Stay tuned. Gift cards will be released today. That helps tremendously. That gets dollars directly in the pockets. Tomorrow the curbside menu comes out. Much love and peace from Brother Luck to you. We're in this together.

As the post went viral, the response fueled my heart to keep fighting, which I did. I was tested in ways I never could have imagined. I had to lay off our entire team while I pivoted. Our massive business debt stormed front and center: loans, payables, credit cards, and payroll. I told my wife, Tina, I had failed: the businesses I was so proud of were shut down.

It is only by the grace of God that Tina and I grew closer while battling our way through the pandemic. My shame was real, but so was my gratitude. Tears flowed as neighbors greeted me at the front door of my house with checks to encourage me, Tina, and our work family. Customers would show up at the restaurant and hand me cash with tears in their eyes. I broke down every time.

In turmoil, I was convinced we would lose it all, but I continually prayed. I guarantee God would not forget my name because I was knocking on his door every day and talking to him whether he had time for me or not. And like a good father, he always did. "Worry about nothing and pray about everything," my uncle had repeatedly encouraged me throughout the years: I wasn't ready to hear his words then, but in the middle of a pandemic, facing inevitable failure, I was.

I'll never forget the fear in my team member's eyes as the uncertainty became real. I cried. I got angry. My tears turned to determination, and I made a decision. We had worked too hard to quit. I needed to pivot. We would survive.

The following two years would require adaptation and improvisation. The bare-knuckle brawl of operating multiple restaurants during the pandemic was brutal: we had to modify our concepts—curbside service, feeding front line workers, and digital streaming, just to name a few.

It was pure exhaustion. Every morning I woke up with new ideas. How would I get us back online? The most successful of these ideas was our online cooking classes. Our teams would assemble three-course cooking kits paired with a bottle of wine. Tina and I would go live on Facebook in our home each night to prepare the cooking kits, knowing you were at home following along. Our vulnerability brought our community into our home; we became connected to you, and you to us while we shared our story during the quarantine.

We had black eyes from more than enough stress and a lack of sleep. But our family showed up: Joe and Shelly, and Mike and Jackie offered a helping hand, washing dishes and taking orders when we couldn't afford to pay any staff. My close friend Nick Lachman cooked by my side for weeks; he volunteered his time and helped me dig our way out of the sinkhole we had fallen in.

There are too many stories to name everyone. Just know that I'm grateful to all of you!

Eventually, our restaurants were allowed to open with limited capacity. We continued to create more opportunities. One of our restaurants, Lucky Dumpling, expanded three times during the shutdown.

As the other businesses in our building shuttered their doors, we absorbed the spaces. We built a new patio with help from volunteers and the Home Builders Association. We opened a bar to increase our capacity and provide more work shifts for our team.

We converted the space above Lucky to a private dining room with a cooking studio to accommodate our many guests who desired an intimate evening with friends and the individual experience that we all love in a dining experience.

Today, my restaurants are thriving.

- *Four by Brother Luck* is busy and defining the cuisine of our region.
- *Lucky Dumpling* has tripled in size and continues to pump out delicious food inspired by my time in Asia and Creole background.
- *The Studio* is still hosting dinners for groups and families searching for that one-of-a-kind experience.

I needed the pandemic to happen. I needed to get my head above water. It was like someone called a much-needed "time out." As the world stopped, so did my travel; and I took the opportunity to reconnect with my people. (And this book would not exist without that pause button.) Sometimes it is necessary to kick the soccer ball backward so you can strategize how to advance the ball and score a goal.

Thank you to everyone who is a part of my story. You have helped me become the man I am today. I look forward to jumping off the next cliff, knowing that you are my safety net below.

ACKNOWLEDGMENTS

Where to even begin? I am grateful for everyone who has contributed to making my dream become a reality. I've always wanted to share my story, and the words on these pages have now made my thoughts eternal.

First and foremost, my highest praise and thanks to God Almighty. Without you, I am nothing.

My wife Tina, who's played the hero in my story repeatedly, thank you. I love you. Your words always encourage me.

To my mom, whom I love dearly: I've always been your first son, and you've always been my mother. Our journeys have taken us apart throughout time, but you were placed in my life for a reason. I love every minute I get to spend with you. I always want to hear more and learn more about you.

To my father, may he rest in peace. Thank you for believing in me and sharing your values with me. I laugh when I think about the television career you always wanted for me. Surprise, I did it!

To my little brother, Slade, whom I love with all my heart: I pray for you every day and cannot wait for us to walk together in Dad's image.

Teri and Steve: thanks for taking a chance on a 16-year-old street kid you hardly knew. From cosigning on my first car and paying my vehicle insurance, you were always there to listen and offer love. God gifted me a second family in you.

My brother-in-law Chris, I love you. Thank you for being there when I needed you. I'll always be there when you need me.

My other brother-in-law Joe, you've become the older brother

I never had. You're a great friend and someone I know will always have my back. To my sister-in-law, Michelle, thank you for letting me live in your home twice. Your family has made such an impact on my life, helping me to discover how much joy can be found in a home. Can I call you sister moving forward?

To my niece Samantha, I miss you and our talks. We love you and will one day speak again.

Thank you to my many mentors and instructors throughout my story, especially Mr. Richard Grausman. I've had some great teachers from all over. You're the ones who inspire me to keep giving back.

To the amazing men who know Jesus and are surrounding me: you pushed me back into God's arms and helped me learn to trust in friendships again.

Thank you to Pastor Soukup for always taking the time to help me see God's plan. My joy and marriage are reflections of the blessings you offered.

Thank you to Marcus Costantino for helping me find my words and becoming my friend along the way. Thank you to Dave Sheets for coordinating all the many pieces to make this book become a reality.

ABOUT THE AUTHORS

Brother Luck

Brother Luck is an award-winning chef, entrepreneur, and advocate for the pursuit of self-discovery. With a childhood marked by humble beginnings, Brother is on a mission to prove to others that while our past is forever a part of who we are, it does not determine the people that we become.

By drawing on his own childhood trauma, Brother uses his life as a testament to prove how pride, courage, determination, and perseverance helped him survive early life challenges and empowered him to achieve great success in the face of adversity.

Today, Brother has earned a reputation as a celebrity chef through appearances on Chopped, Beat Bobby Flay, and Top Chef, and also as a successful business owner with the establishment of his restaurants Four by Brother Luck and Lucky Dumpling. He lives in Colorado with his wife, Tina.

Marcus Costantino

Marcus is a business and non-profit leader, consultant, writer, and literary agent. Following five years in sales and marketing in corporate America, he worked seventeen years at the Glen Eyrie Conference Center, a ministry of The Navigators.

As a business consultant and writer, he helps influencers strategically position themselves in the marketplace; and it usually starts with a book. His literary and writing portfolio includes a US Congressman and various non-profit executives. He is also the editor-in-chief at Believers Book Services.

His books include *Igniting Your Influence: 21 Speakers, Coaches, Leaders, and Experts help you write your first Book* and *What's Next? Talking with God about the Rest of Your Life*. Marcus, and his wife Trista, live in Colorado.

APPENDIX

I Got Your Back Project
Changing the culture surrounding mental health.
www.igotyourback.info

Culinary Hospitality Outreach Wellness
CHOW's mission is to support wellness within the hospitality industry and to improve the lives of our community through shared stories, skills, and resources. www.chowco.org

Not 9 to 5
A non-profit global leader in mental health advocacy for the foodservice and hospitality sector. Through practical education and meaningful community-building, we are reimagining the industry by breaking stigmas and fueling hope. www.not9to5.org

Children of Restaurant Employees
Children of Restaurant Employees provides financial relief to food and beverage service employees with children when navigating a qualifying circumstance. www.coregives.org

APPENDIX

I Got Your Back Project
Changing the culture surrounding mental health.
www.igotyourback.info

Culinary Hospitality Outreach Wellness
CHOW's mission is to support wellness within the hospitality industry and to improve the lives of our community through shared stories, skills, and resources. www.chowco.org

Not 9 to 5
A non-profit global leader in mental health advocacy for the foodservice and hospitality sector. Through practical education and meaningful community-building, we are reimagining the industry by breaking stigmas and fueling hope. www.not9to5.org

Children of Restaurant Employees
Children of Restaurant Employees provides financial relief to food and beverage service employees with children when navigating a qualifying circumstance. www.coregives.org

SCRIPTURE REFERENCES

Dedication: 1 Corinthians 13:4-8

Introduction: Proverbs 27:17 As iron sharpens iron, so one person sharpens another.

Chapter 1: Proverbs 24:10 If you faint in the day of adversity, your strength is small. (ESV)

Chapter 2: Proverbs 20:20 If one curses his father or his mother, his lamp will be put out in utter darkness. (ESV)

Chapter 3: Proverbs 11:14 Where there is no guidance the people fall, But in abundance of counselors there is victory. (NASB)

Chapter 4: Proverbs 9:9 Give instruction to a wise man and he will be still wiser; teach a righteous man, and he will increase in learning. (ESV)

Chapter 5: Proverbs 31: 8-9 Speak up for those who cannot speak for themselves, for the rights of all who are destitute. Speak up and judge fairly; defend the rights of the poor and needy.

Chapter 6: Proverbs 22:6 Train up a child in the way he should go; even when he is old he will not depart from it. (ESV)

Chapter 7: Proverbs 15:13 A happy heart makes the face cheerful, but heartache crushes the spirit.

Chapter 8: Proverbs 13:20 Whoever walks with the wise becomes wise, but the companion of fools will suffer harm. (ESV)

Chapter 9: Proverbs 20:28 Love and faithfulness keep a king safe; through love his throne is made secure.

Chapter 10: Proverbs 23:3 Do not crave his delicacies for that food is deceptive.

Chapter 11: Proverbs 4:23 Above all else, guard your heart, for everything you do flows from it.

Chapter 12: Proverbs 21:3 To do what is right and just is more acceptable to the Lord than sacrifice.

Chapter 13: Proverbs 19:20 Listen to advice and accept discipline, and at the end you will be counted among the wise.

Chapter 14: Proverbs 15:21 Folly is a joy to him who lacks sense, but a man of understanding walks straight ahead. (ESV)

Chapter 15: Proverbs 10:13 Wisdom is found on the lips of the discerning, but a rod is for the back of one who has no sense.

Chapter 16: Proverbs 23:4-5 Do not wear yourself out to get rich; do not trust your own cleverness. Cast but a glance at riches, and they are gone, for they will surely sprout wings and fly off to the sky like an eagle.

Chapter 17: Proverbs 14:23 All hard work brings a profit, but mere talk leads only to poverty.

Chapter 18: Proverbs 27:1 Do not boast about tomorrow, for you do not know what a day may bring.

Chapter 19: Proverbs 29:11 Fools give full vent to their rage, but the wise bring calm in the end.

Chapter 20: Proverbs 1:5 Let the wise hear and increase in learning, and the one who understands obtain guidance... (ESV)

Chapter 21: Proverbs 10:1 The proverbs of Solomon: A wise son brings joy to his father, but a foolish son brings grief to his mother.

Chapter 22: Proverbs 3:27 Do not withhold good from those to whom it is due, when it is in your power to act.

Chapter 23: Proverbs 8:33 Listen to my instruction and be wise; do not disregard it.

Chapter 24: Proverbs 18:1 Whoever isolates himself seeks his own desire; he breaks out against all sound judgment. (ESV)

Chapter 25: Proverbs 18:22 He who finds a wife finds what is good and receives favor from the LORD.

NOTES

2. SHATTERED SOUL

1. Eldredge, John, Wild at Heart: Discovering the Secret of a Man's Soul. (New York: Thomas Nelson, 2006), 72.

4. HOW DID YOU GET STARTED AS A CHEF?

1. Long co-chaired by chef Marcus Samuelsson, Careers through Culinary Arts Program (C-CAP) is a workforce development nonprofit that provides underserved teens a pathway to success. Annually, C-CAP provides culinary, job, and life skills to over 20,000 middle and high school students in seven regions across the United States: New York City, Newark, Philadelphia and Camden, Chicago, Los Angeles, Washington DC/Maryland/Northern Virginia and Arizona, including seven Navajo Reservation schools. www.ccapinc.org

5. WILL CHEF BROTHER LUCK PLEASE STAND?

1. While he was alive, James Beard always welcomed students, authors, chefs, and other food and beverage professionals into his home—his kitchen was truly at the heart of America's burgeoning twentieth century food scene. On November 5, 1986, the James Beard Foundation officially opened the James Beard House "to provide a center for the culinary arts and to continue to foster the interest James Beard inspired in all aspects of food, its preparation presentation, and of course, enjoyment," according to a press release issued that day. www.jamesbeard.org
2. https://health.usnews.com/wellness/mind/articles/2018-10-26/michael-phelps-gets-real-about-mental-illness
3. https://www.insider.com/michael-phelps-weight-of-gold-olympians-suicide-depression-epidemic-2020-7, (last accessed 4/21/2023)
4. https://olympics.com/ioc/news/mental-health-matters-helping-athletes-to-stay-mentally-fit, (last accessed 4/21/2023)

6. CHEFS WERE NOT MY ONLY MENTORS

1. Slim, Iceberg, Pimp: The Story of my Life, Trade Paperback Edition: May 2011. (New York: Cash Money Content, an imprint of Simon & Shuster)
2. Ibid.
3. "What has been will be again, what has been done will be done again; there is nothing new under the sun." (Ecclesiastes 1:9)

8. HALFRICAN

1. https://www.vice.com/en/article/j5b7wk/brother-luck-race, (last accessed 4/21/2022)
2. Ibid.
3. www.danakeithfilm.com

13. ROCKY MOUNTAIN HIGH

1. Eldredge, John, Wild at Heart: Discoverining the Secret of a Man's Soul. (New York: Thomas Nelson, 2006), 104.

17. POP-UP DINNERS

1. www.chefbluck.blogspot.com, (2008 – 2013)

20. A MOTHER'S COIN

1. Mission: The Gohan Society's mission is to advocate for a mutual appreciation of culinary heritage between the United States and Japan through outreach to chefs, culinary arts professionals, and food enthusiasts. Through cultural and gastronomic education and exchange, chefs, food and wine professionals, and those interested in the unique sensibility of Japanese culinary traditions, we hope to inspire and enrich their artistry, as well as their cultural understanding.
   The Gohan Society serves as a resource for traditional Japanese food culture and cuisine--the ingredients, techniques and methods of food production, and serves as a catalyst for the expansion of that knowledge. gohansociety.org
2. https://totalfood.com/c-cap-alumni-chef-awarded-culinary-exchange-scholarships-japan-china